"If you ever feel like you are drowning in the negative cycles of your own thought, this is the book for you. Alicia Muñoz provides a detailed description of this debilitating phenomenon, and an equally detailed description of the process of moving from rumination to engagement and connection. We recommend a careful reading and practice of the liberating processes."

—**Harville Hendrix, PhD**, and **Helen**
coauthors of *Getting the Love You Wa*

"Alicia Muñoz is a true artist—in how she sees the nuances of relationships and in how she helps readers address the complexities in simple yet effective ways. It doesn't hurt that she draws us in with writing that's at once compassionate, direct, and utterly engaging."

Livia Kent, MFA,
editor in chief of *Psychotherapy Networker*

"Relationship rumination is an unrecognized issue and a major problem in couples therapy, and this book gives a clear map to see a way through. Alicia Muñoz's SLOW process is easy to follow and makes intimacy an adventure. Everyone contemplating a relationship should read this book, and every therapist trying to help couples out of conflict and into a loving connection needs to know these exercises."

—**Tammy Nelson, PhD,**
TEDx speaker, and author of *Open Monogamy*

"Muñoz describes the pervasiveness of overthinking, outlines its destructive nature between partners, and offers tools to replace overthinking with presence. Rumination's devastation often unfolds because people are unaware of these tendencies, and this book gently invites the reader to consider their own origins of rumination. She outlines the SLOW strategy of seeing, labeling, opening, and welcoming as an effective alternative to rumination. This is a must-read for everyone in a relationship!"

—**Lori Brotto, PhD**, Canada Research Chair in women's sexual
health, and professor at the University of British Columbia

"This tender, insightful, and well-written book will help you recognize and break the habit of overthinking—'the cheapest and most accessible mind-altering substance' there is. Alicia's profound practice of SLOW (seeing, labeling, opening, and welcoming) is a concrete tool to help couples reduce their anxiety by helping them understand their internal experiences rather than defending against them. This practice will transform your relationships and your own well-being."

—**Jillian Pransky**, author of *Deep Listening*

"It's so hard to accept that our thoughts about our partner are often neither true nor helpful. Blending research, practical advice, and case studies, Alicia Muñoz shows how you can deal with these blaming, worrying, doubting, controlling, or self-pitying ruminations. She offers readers practical, inspiring guidance through the SLOW technique and other tools to enable them to reap the benefits of connection, healthy boundaries, and safety in love."

—**Gleb Tsipursky, PhD**, cutting-edge expert in
relationship science; and author of the global best seller,
The Blindspots Between Us

"If you've ever experienced the ways that incessant worrying can erode the foundation of a relationship or undermine your self-confidence, then you'll appreciate Alicia Muñoz's straightforward guide to slowing down, reconnecting to yourself and others, and finally resolving whatever might be causing your anxious mind to go into overdrive. Those thoughts will become a gift—once you learn how to unwrap them and use what's inside to reclaim your power."

—**Neil Sattin**, host of the *Relationship Alive* podcast

"Many clients struggle with rumination and making up stories about themselves and their partners, which ultimately undermines their relationships and well-being. With many helpful analogies, client examples, and concrete exercises, this is a very accessible handbook to help couples move through these deteriorating patterns. Instead of allowing anxiety and the illusion of control to run relationships, Alicia Muñoz deftly teaches how to build relationships based on choice, clarity, emotional availability, awareness, and teamwork."

—**Jennifer Gunsaullus, PhD**, sociologist, intimacy coach, international speaker, and author of *From Madness to Mindfulness*

"Once again, Alicia Muñoz delivers on her promise to help us bring more care and awareness to our intimate relationships. In *Stop Overthinking Your Relationship*, she skillfully and wisely unpacks one of the most pervasive, pernicious, and poorly understood problems in relationships—destructive, ruminative, out-of-control thinking. Readers will see themselves on these pages and benefit immensely from her brilliance and generosity."

—**Alexandra H. Solomon, PhD**, professor and licensed clinical psychologist at Northwestern University, author of *Loving Bravely* and *Taking Sexy Back*, and host of the *Reimagining Love* podcast

"Anxiety and overthinking cloud the lens through which we view and experience our relationships, often fueling disconnection and challenges that, left unchecked, become increasingly difficult to overcome. In this book, Alicia Muñoz blends her expertise and vast experience to peel back the curtain on anxious overthinking, illustrate the overt and nuanced ways it affects relationships, and, importantly, she shares tools and practices that reveal a clear path to more understanding, connection, and love."

> —**Jodi Richardson, PhD**, international anxiety and well-being speaker; best-selling author of *Anxious Kids* and *Anxious Mums*; and host of the podcast, *Well, hello anxiety*

"Alicia Muñoz's *Stop Overthinking Your Relationship* highlights the problem of relationship rumination—and charts a path toward healthier relationships.... Muñoz knows that this kind of change takes courage. Her friendly approach is vital: she portrays a persistent belief in positive change. The result is the compelling gift through which both partners will be able to be themselves, making relationship growth an adventure."

> —*Foreword Reviews*

Stop

OVERTHINKING

Your

Relationship

Break the Cycle of Anxious Rumination to Nurture Love, Trust & Connection with Your Partner

ALICIA MUÑOZ, LPC

New Harbinger Publications, Inc.

Publisher's Note

This publication is designed to provide accurate and authoritative information in regard to the subject matter covered. It is sold with the understanding that the publisher is not engaged in rendering psychological, financial, legal, or other professional services. If expert assistance or counseling is needed, the services of a competent professional should be sought.

NEW HARBINGER PUBLICATIONS is a registered trademark of New Harbinger Publications, Inc.

New Harbinger Publications is an employee-owned company.

New Harbinger Publications, Inc.
5674 Shattuck Avenue
Oakland, CA 94609
www.newharbinger.com

Cover design by Amy Daniel

Acquired by Elizabeth Hollis Hansen

Edited by Gretel Hakanson

FSC
www.fsc.org
MIX
Paper from responsible sources
FSC® C011935

Library of Congress Cataloging-in-Publication Data

Names: Muñoz, Alicia (Licensed Professional Counselor), author.
Title: Stop overthinking your relationship : break the cycle of anxious rumination to nurture love, trust, and connection with your partner / Alicia Muñoz, LPC.
Description: Oakland, CA : New Harbinger Publications, [2022] | Includes biblio-graphical references.
Identifiers: LCCN 2022020549 | ISBN 9781648480034 (trade paperback)
Subjects: LCSH: Man-woman relationships. | Couples--Psychology. | Interpersonal relations. | BISAC: FAMILY & RELATIONSHIPS / Marriage & Long-Term Relationships | PSYCHOLOGY / Psychotherapy / Couples & Family
Classification: LCC HQ801 .M8449 2022 | DDC 646.7/7--dc23/eng/20220520
LC record available at https://lccn.loc.gov/2022020549

Printed in the United States of America

24   23   22

10   9   8   7   6   5   4   3   2   1   First Printing

To my husband, Mike, and my son, Lucas—
nothing tops being with you.

Contents

Foreword

Alicia Muñoz sets the bar for writing honest, helpful, and informative books that are also engaging and true. I am struck by her wisdom and heartened by her simple honesty in describing her struggles. She is a wise, insightful, and compassionate clinician and person. She doesn't try to conceal her challenges but instead models the rewards of conscious love in a very real way.

Even writing this foreword helped me make a shift in my own relationship after I'd read only a few pages. A nasty storm was raging over our town. The ground around our house, saturated by days of rain, released its grip on the roots of an Oregon white oak, which promptly toppled over and crashed onto our porch. As the storm howled overhead, my husband went outside to saw branches and painstakingly remove the broken tree. It took him most of the day. At last, he stuck his head through the door to tell me he was almost done. When I went outside to see his work, I noticed that the tree was gone. Even the muddy ground had been cleaned up. But what I homed in on at that moment was that the shovel and wheelbarrow were still in the yard.

I remember thinking to myself, *That stuff shouldn't be there. Why can't he put things away when he's finished? He should be more conscientious.* Even though he'd been heroically schlepping in the storm for hours to save our porch, my thoughts had focused on what he had *not* done.

And then I got it—instantly. I was ruminating about what was wrong. What Alicia calls a rumination cycle had started spinning—in my case, a hybrid of control and blame. My husband's little oversight had commandeered my attention. I was like a cat who licks a sore paw and so irritates the wound. Luckily, I *saw* it, and so I was able to stop carping on my husband's negligence and pivot into appreciating the hard work he had put into the tree removal for both of our benefit.

Alicia's metaphors are striking; she compares relationship rumination to what Apple users call the "spinning beach ball of death"—a path that goes round and round with no exit ramp to stop it except awareness of your own thinking and behavior. I've become more aware of my own spinning beach ball after reading this extraordinary and relatable book.

As a frequent writer and speaker on the topic of relationships, I describe love as a feeling and loving as a skill set. In *Stop Overthinking Your Relationship*, Alicia focuses on essential (and learnable) skills for loving well, both in and out of a committed relationship. One of the foundational skills is cultivating a growth mindset. From there, in her exploration of five "attachment style pairings," she offers a fresh perspective on attachment style dynamics in love relationships and looks at how unchecked rumination fuels both anxious and avoidant attachment.

Alicia's essential message is that we *can* change the plot of our love stories. One way to do this—and undo rumination—is by learning how to be with the things we typically and chronically avoid. Using a simple, elegant practice she sums up with the acronym SLOW, which stands for seeing, labeling, opening, and welcoming, she offers a concrete tool for counteracting the conditioning that has turned many of us into spectacular overthinkers in love. The powerful concepts packed into this memorable four-letter acronym form the basis of every effective mindfulness approach I know.

In the end, it's not our differences that make or break our relationships but our interpersonal skills—skills we can practice to effectively navigate our troubles. These skills can even turn some of our troubles into gifts. With humor and warmth, *Stop Overthinking Your Relationship* delivers essential information on reducing rumination and creating a loving relationship to anyone willing to pick it up, follow its suggestions, and slow down.

—Linda Carroll, therapist and author of *Love Skills:
The Keys to Unlocking Lasting, Wholehearted Love*

Love's Quiet Enemy

Once upon a time, two people fell in love.

Together, they traveled, shared meals, went on adventures, had sex, talked, cried, fought, made up, and revealed fears and longings. Here, I'll name these people You and Me.

You was confident, though unmotivated, so being around Me inspired and energized You, providing a sense of purpose. Me was ambitious, though socially reserved, so being around You helped Me relax and take risks. As a couple, for a while, they felt complete.

After several months, they moved in together. Me received a promotion and worked late. You made lots of plans with friends. They touched less, talked less, and ate meals on the fly. They got busy, looked at their phones, started sleeping in separate beds, and rarely had time for adventures or trips. They worried about the future, controlled each other, and doubted their love. They grew resentful. It didn't look like they were going to make it, as a couple.

I wish I could say the plotline of this story is unusual. But it's not. I hear it often, as a couples therapist, even when the details are different. So how do love stories with passionate, hopeful beginnings like this go wrong? Here's how: couples get derailed by overthinking.

In romantic relationships, overthinking gradually—day after day, month after month—interferes with a couple's access to essential relational resources and skills. It shortens their bandwidth for awareness, empathy, curiosity, and whatever is happening in their own hearts. Basically, overthinking turns into a bad cognitive habit.

It starts with a thought. This thought—an opinion, misinterpretation, prediction, or judgment—leads to more thoughts. Perhaps some of these examples may be familiar to you. When one partner comes home late, the other one thinks, *They're neglecting me. Work is more important than I am.* If one of them doesn't initiate lovemaking, the other one thinks, *We're on our way to a sexless marriage. I knew this would happen.* If one of them is distracted at the dinner table, the other one thinks, *They're bored. They have nothing to say to me. I can't believe it's come to this.* If one of them forgets to ask a follow-up question after a doctor's visit, the other one thinks, *They're selfish and insensitive. I'm alone in this relationship.*

If thoughts like these arise when a partner feels threatened, then similar thoughts may follow. Reflexive, negative thoughts fueled by anxiety don't just pop up and go away. They multiply. They may even become thought-pinwheels, spinning into what is known as *rumination* in the mental health world. Each partner's ruminative thoughts distort their perceptions of their mate. Over time, as the distortions build into stories about the other person, partners stop opening up, relating directly, and sharing themselves. They lose touch with the adventure of love.

It's hard to blame couples who, like the two people in this story, find themselves losing hope in their relationship due to overthinking. In our workplaces, schools, and communities, thinking is valued more than openness to experience. Thinking is viewed as our most valuable human asset, the mainspring of civilization, culture, art, psychology, science, and literature. As a result, many of us are skilled overthinkers by the time we enter romantic relationships.

Love and life are uncertain. When we can't predict the future, don't know the solution to a problem, or get overwhelmed, filtering our experiences through stories and narratives gives us a sense of agency and control. In a culture where thinking is glorified, it becomes the cheapest and most accessible mind-altering substance. Naturally, overthinking tends to be a couple's go-to coping strategy when partners get scared, feel lost, or can't figure out what to do.

In my therapy practice, I've seen overthinking erode love between people whenever it operates unseen and unchallenged. My vantage point isn't solely professional either. As a former chronic ruminator with a preference for doubt and self-pity cycles, I've suffered the destructive effects of overthinking firsthand. Following a painful divorce in my late twenties, I didn't have much faith in healthy partnerships or in my ability to be in one myself. Now, over two decades later, I know differently. Happy love stories are created, not stumbled upon. Not only have I lived the changes that come with undoing rumination in the relationship my husband and I have developed over the last seventeen years, but I've also helped hundreds of couples foster deeper intimacy and safer, more fulfilling connections by doing this work.

If you've picked up this book, chances are you've seen the damage anxious overthinking can do in a relationship. If so, you're in the right place to learn a better way.

How Relationship Rumination Works Against You

Have you ever observed a colorful little beach ball pop up on your computer screen, usually when something has gone wrong? Macintosh users refer to it as the Spinning Beach Ball of Death—or sometimes the Marble of Doom. If you've witnessed this endlessly spinning rainbow pinwheel in action, you know it's a sign of trouble. You may have to force quit your software program and lose some of your recent work. You could end up spending hours on the phone with tech support. The Spinning Beach Ball of Death is a nifty metaphor for overthinking.

When overthinking interrupts the natural flow of your life, it's also a sign of trouble. Unlike a beach ball, rumination cycles aren't colorful. They're dreary and predictable, made up of repetitive negative thoughts instead of rainbow colors. The more they spin, the more space they take up in your mind. They can spin so fast and take up so much space that it gets hard to see past them. It's easy to fall into the trap of assuming their anxiety-provoking content is true.

When you ruminate, your attention and energy get syphoned off into repetitive negative thinking. The catch with doing it in a relationship is this: Overthinking doesn't only deplete and squander *your* attention and energy. It affects your partner too. Although rumination cycles seem to occur privately in your own mind, they spin in a relational field you both cocreate.

Overthinking has an impact, regardless of whether it happens in one mind or two. It stokes frustrations and insecurities and influences communication and behavior. If partners spin dual (you might call them "dueling") rumination cycles, troubles will intensify. Each person risks seeing the other through a haze of negativity. Caught in the crossfire created by the negative emotional charge of dueling rumination cycles, partners bristle and grow defensive.

I use the term *relationship rumination* to describe this type of overthinking. In co-rumination—a related concept—two people ruminate together about the same thing. Relationship rumination is a broader term meant to describe a general pattern of repetitive, negative overthinking engaged in by one or both partners that erodes trust and sabotages love. In this book, I'll use the terms rumination, overthinking, repetitive negative thinking, passive thinking, and relationship rumination to describe variations of the same phenomenon: passive, unwanted overthinking that happens so much and so often it erodes a couple's bond.

Rumination has been linked to eating disorders, anxiety, depression, PTSD, substance abuse disorders, and OCD. Not only is it a symptom of unhappiness; it's also a cause. A 2013 study of 32,827 people done by the University of Liverpool in England exposes rumination as a higher predictor of mental health problems than biological factors, social factors, or traumatic life events (Kinderman et al. 2013). Tough life events, a history of mental illness, poverty, and interpersonal problems lead to poorer mental health. At the same time, these things lead there indirectly: *through* rumination. In other words, circumstances become serious mental health problems only when we can't stop thinking about them in unhealthy ways.

This isn't merely an interesting fact supported by research. If rumination leads to depression and anxiety, then decreasing it can do the opposite: increase your well-being. You can't change your past or your genetic makeup, but you can change how much you ruminate. This isn't to say you should ignore painful circumstances. That would promote mental illness by denying reality. But if you can channel your energies into more helpful coping strategies and thinking styles, you have a better chance of overcoming obstacles. A systematic review of nineteen studies focused on reducing rumination conducted between 2002 and 2012 found that mindfulness-based and cognitive behavioral interventions can effectively help reduce rumination (Querstret and Cropley 2013). Less rumination leads to happier love stories.

When overthinking combines with the emotionally charged needs and fears in an intimate adult bond, you can end up reliving the same conflict with your partner over the course of many years—though it may disguise itself in novel forms. You may even hear some couples talk about having the same fight they had on their first date a decade later.

Awareness of your repetitive negative thinking can reduce the intensity of conflicts—or even defuse them completely. The differences between partners don't make or break a relationship. What *does* is how partners think about these differences.

How to Use This Book

If you can't see how something hurts you, it's easier to keep doing it. Many couples don't see how rumination erodes their connection. This book will help you recognize the toll overthinking takes so you can reconnect with what matters most.

In the first chapter, you'll explore relationship rumination in depth— what it is, why it's overlooked, and how it ties into early attachment fears. In chapter 2, you'll dive into the concept of a relationship field along with your attachment style pairing—or ASP. In chapters 3 through 7, you'll get to know your mindset and identify your thoughts, rumination cycles, triggers, warning lights, and dead-end scripts. You'll also be introduced to SLOW, a four-step practice that can help you shift from *thinking about* what's upsetting you to *being with* what's happening in the moment. SLOW stands for seeing, labeling, opening, and welcoming.

In chapter 8, you'll review practical tips for applying and using SLOW. In chapter 9, you'll learn important preventive, palliative, and curative relationship care skills to nurture your bond. You'll also create your own personalized relationship first aid kit. Exercises will guide you to reflect on and apply the skills you'll be mastering here to your own life.

Ten different couples' stories have been woven through these chapters. They're meant to highlight problems arising from relationship rumination as well as ways of handling them. Although I've drawn them from my work as a therapist, the couples featured in these pages are fictional. Take what serves you from their struggles and successes and disregard what doesn't.

Most of the exercises in this book invite you to write responses or track thoughts. I recommend you get a blank journal for this purpose so you have everything in one place and can easily revisit it later. The quizzes, prompts, and assessments you'll find in these pages are not diagnostic tools. They're meant to guide you and stimulate reflection. You'll find worksheet versions of most of the exercises online at http://www.newharbinger.com/50034.

If you're single, you'll benefit from practicing SLOW and working through the solo and joint exercises on your own (these can be done alone with slight adjustments). Focus on your relationship with yourself and examine the role overthinking has played in past relationships.

Moments of overwhelm, frustration, and anxiety are inevitable when you're learning new things, looking at patterns, reflecting on yourself, and exploring your personal history. If you and your partner do this work together, do it in your own way and at your own pace. I encourage what I call "adult time-outs" (more on these in chapter 9), as a form of palliative relationship care. Take adult time-outs if you find yourselves disagreeing or arguing. You'll probably have different motivation levels for reading chapters, doing exercises, and using tools and techniques. That's totally normal. Taking an adult time-out means separating from each other for a brief time. This can help you shift your attention away from a conflict, regain perspective, and calm down.

Mishandling vulnerable information your partner reveals in trusting moments, or using it as proof of negative beliefs or judgments, won't help either of you. Shaming, punishing, manipulating, or controlling your partner undermines safety, making it harder to share and collaborate. If you catch yourself engaging in these or any other relationship-sabotaging behaviors, take responsibility for your missteps and repair. Skip ahead to chapter 9, if you need to, and read about what goes into a successful repair so you can start practicing it now.

Discomfort isn't always a bad thing. Difficult feelings, sensations, impulses, and insights *will* arise when you no longer rely on relationship rumination to bring relief in anxiety-provoking situations. Some of what surfaces will be unsettling. This is because exploration is risky. When you face aspects of yourself you've avoided, denied, or buried under repetitive negative thinking, there are bound to be risks.

But avoiding exploration is also risky. In Helen Keller's words, "Avoiding danger is no safer in the long run than outright exposure. The fearful are caught as often as the bold" (Keller 1940, 51). In other words, ignoring relationship rumination isn't a safe choice either. Overthinking in your relationship carries its own set of costs, risks, and consequences. These may include anxiety, joylessness, a nagging sense of something missing, and existential angst. Doing what you've always done because you've always done it fuels disconnection, resentment, and unhappiness. The goal isn't *avoiding* discomfort. It's getting to the root of your relationship problems while remaining curious, open, and connected through difficult moments.

If there's abuse, mental illness, trauma, or addiction in your relationship, seek trusted guidance and support. In some cases, mood or attention deficit disorders may interfere with your ability to do certain practices and exercises. If you've felt sad, fearful, irritable, forgetful, hopeless, or unmotivated for more than a few weeks in a row, consider talking with a therapist or other mental health professional. No self-help book can be a stand-in for supportive mental health treatment, couples therapy, or psychopharmacology when that's what you need.

If you and your partner have little or no foundation of safety in your relationship, be honest with yourself about where you are. As long as hostility interferes with caring, respectful speaking and listening, digging deeper without a professional guiding you can backfire and fuel conflicts. The same goes for strong-arming your partner into working through this book when they don't want to. Instead, work through it separately. Consider revisiting the joint exercises together later. Or else make peace with working through this book on your own without your partner's active participation. Understanding more about relationship rumination and doing the exercises and practices on your own can still benefit you greatly as a couple.

Intentional Speaking and Listening

When we speak to people in our everyday lives, we usually focus on conveying information or eliciting the response we want. In everyday speaking and listening, it's also common to multitask as we share and listen. We talk into a headset while pushing a grocery cart and scanning shelves. We respond to emails during a lecture. We ring up items on a cash register while chatting about the weather. We navigate traffic as our partner relays an anecdote. Our attention is divided.

Intentional speaking and listening is different from what you do when you communicate with other people while you're multitasking. In this book's joint exercises, you'll be invited to assume the roles of Speaker and Listener. The Speaker-Listener format has been a core component of cognitive-behavioral couple therapy (CBCT) for several decades and before that, of behavioral couple therapy (BCT; Baucom et al. 2015). When your entire focus is on sharing reflections or on listening to what your partner shares, your attention is qualitatively different than normal. Below, you'll find a list of your responsibilities for each role.

Responsibilities When Speaking

Share *you*. Don't talk *about* yourself (as if you were reporting). Instead, share what's rooted in your body—what's true for you right now. Don't withhold what's vulnerable or uncomfortable for you to admit. Risk disclosing your imperfections and flaws.

Own your reality. If something your partner says or does sets off a defensive reaction or a mental pinwheel of negative thoughts, reorient your attention to the here and now. Resist the temptation to slip into theories or stories *about* your partner, unless you preface them with "What I make up about you is…" or "The story I tell myself about you is…" Keep the focus on yourself when you speak, using I-statements. Connect with what's happening inside you right now (for example, "I feel, my interpretation is, I have an impulse to, I'm conscious of...").

Remain present focused rather than past or future focused. It's harder to get caught up in rumination cycles of blame, control, worry, doubt, or self-pity when you're in the present. If thoughts spin, try to see the content of these thoughts and to recognize them as thoughts. If you're sharing about something that happened in the past, pay attention to how you're experiencing your recollection of it in your body *now*.

Let yourself *not* know. Share open-ended, personal reflections over absolute truths and certainties. Allow yourself not to know rather than presenting yourself as all-knowing.

Responsibilities When Listening

Ground yourself. Quiet your own mental chatter, stories, interpretations, and ruminative thinking by sensing where your body makes contact with the chair or the floor. Remind yourself of your partner's fundamental goodness and humanity. Remain humble when you're tempted to believe you know more about who they are than they do. Resist the urge to criticize, judge, nitpick, negate, control, or dismiss. Notice and release the impulse to listen selectively or distort your partner's words to reinforce a cherished opinion you hold of them.

Focus your full attention on your partner. When you get distracted by your own thoughts or reactions, recommit to your role as Listener.

Remain curious. There's always more to your partner than meets the eye. Listen with an open mind.

Trust and stay in the process. Settle into the unknown of whatever is emerging, as unsettling as this may feel. Surrender control for the time being. Allow what's true and real in this one moment you're living to be enough.

Sometimes, what your partner shares will raise your anxiety. If this happens, make a mental note of it: *I'm feeling some anxiety.* Do what you can to soothe yourself (you'll learn ways to do this in upcoming chapters). Avoid jumping to conclusions, fixing things, rescuing your partner, or seeing their discomfort as your issue to solve. In the role of Listener, you support your partner by being with them as they are, without trying to change them.

Thinking About vs. Being With

I'm going to invite you to make a small but radical shift in how you approach internal and external experiences—particularly the ones that set off rumination cycles. You'll be pivoting from *thinking about* moments that unsettle you to *being with* them.

Most of our *thinking about* muscles are overdeveloped. In contrast, our *being with* muscles are underused. If our ability to *think about* our experiences were represented by one leg and our ability to *be with* our experiences were represented by the other, most of us would hop around like kids doing potato-sack races. Our *thinking about* legs would be over-sized and hypermuscular, while our *being with* legs would be puny and feeble.

Being with events, others, and our own emotions, sensations, and impulses isn't something most of us have been explicitly taught how to do. When an event takes you off guard and you feel something emotionally or physically unnerving, do you consciously spend time *being with* your inner experience? If your answer is no, then you're a normal twenty-first century human. Most of us don't consciously choose to *be with* unsettling experiences. Instead, we try to get rid of them. Or else we assume our ability to be with all of our experiences is a given, like our ability to breathe. Except it isn't. *Being with* is a capacity.

The thinking messages we received as children turn us into adults who struggle to be with ourselves, people, events, and experiences we don't understand or aren't prepared for. Modern-day technology doesn't help us develop our *being with* capacity, either. It puts our thinking on hyperdrive with powerful devices that do many wonderful things but can also stoke our relationship rumination.

With the help of advanced technology, we've gotten good at thinking about, solving, and managing increasingly complex problems and relationships. At the same time, we've become people who don't always know how to *be with* ourselves and others. We've become chronically purposeful. With so much to do—and to think about—we don't have much time to be with the rich kaleidoscope of experiences that make up our inner world.

Why is this a problem in romantic relationships? When we can't really *be with* feelings and experiences, we lose our natural attunement to ourselves, our partners, and our lives. Despite living in close quarters, even loving couples end up feeling lonely, misunderstood, and isolated from one another. Their shrunken *being with* capacity imprisons them within their own private, invisible thought-bubbles of fear, worry, judgment, and insecurity.

Being with yourself and your partner is a radical act.

Shifting from *thinking about* to *being with* can help you see when you're hopping around on overthinking so you can shift your weight to *being*. Doing this regularly will strengthen your *being with* muscles and help you achieve more balance. Over time, you'll toggle more flexibly between *thinking about* and *being with* a wider range of experiences in the here and now.

Maybe you can already sense the difference between these two approaches. When you *think about* something upsetting, you create distance between you and what you're thinking about. You generate more thoughts about it. But this distancing strategy has a cost. Even if your thoughts are interesting and engaging, they're not the same thing as direct experience. Distancing yourself from reality with repetitive, negative thinking feeds rumination.

When you choose to *be with* experiences, you get closer to what's uncomfortable for you. You also get closer to life. The embodied knowing you gain from a direct connection to what's happening in the present can bring all aspects of you into alignment far more so than repetitive, negative thoughts.

SOLO EXERCISE: Making the Shift

In a journal, make two columns and label them: "Thinking About" and "Being With." Under the "Thinking About" column, write "I'm thinking about" followed by a brief description of something that upset you in your relationship recently. You might write, "my partner's grumpiness" in the "Thinking About" column. Then, under the "Being With" column, write "I'm being with" followed by the same brief description of the same event.

Repeat this process a few times with different situations or events that have upset you. When you're done, read the first sentence you wrote under the "Thinking About" column aloud. Notice how it feels to link this upsetting item with the *thinking about* approach. Then, read the sentence you wrote under the "Being With" column aloud. Notice how it feels to link this upsetting item with the *being with* approach.

See if you can pick up on any subtle differences between these two approaches when you pair them with each upsetting item. For a PDF worksheet of this exercise, go to http://www.newharbinger.com/50034.

SOLO EXERCISE: Being and Thinking Messages Checklist

As children, we were taught life lessons by parents, caregivers, teachers, authorities, and the media. This exercise will help you perceive whether you were taught to mostly *be with* your experiences or to mostly *think about* them.

In a journal, organize the messages you received under two columns, one titled "Being Messages," the other titled "Thinking Messages." You may have received these messages directly, through spoken words or commands, or indirectly, through behaviors you saw modeled by important people in your life. Write down any additional messages you received related to being or thinking under the appropriate heading. For a PDF worksheet of this exercise, go to http://www.newharbinger.com/50034.

Being Messages	Thinking Messages
Just be.	Think before you act.
Stay with sensations.	Think before you speak.
Notice what you feel.	Think ahead.
Let yourself sense.	Who do you think you are?
Trust the process.	What do you think you're doing?
Focus your attention inward.	Be thoughtful.
Allow what's happening.	Think carefully.
Learning takes patience.	Be prepared for everything.
Make space for what's arising.	Think about the future.
Tune in to yourself with kindness.	Think back on what happened.
Accept all of yourself.	Let me do the thinking.
Discomfort is normal.	What are you, dumb?
Rest in the experience.	You'd better think ahead.
Be present without avoiding or fixing it.	Solve the problem.

JOINT EXERCISE: Reflections on Being and Thinking

Review the "Being and Thinking Messages Checklist." and circle the top three thinking messages you received growing up. Reflect on the following questions or write your answers in a journal. If you like, share what you've dis-covered, referring to the Speaker and Listener responsibilities above.

* What did you notice about the number of "being messages" you received as compared to "thinking messages"?

* Do you remember where, or from whom, you got each of the three messages you circled?

* Do you remember when each of these messages was imparted (your age)?

* How has each of these messages impacted your approach to relationship challenges?

You may be wondering, *Won't a book on overthinking make us over-think our relationship more than we already do?* Some version of this type of concern usually precedes challenging the status quo or making a change. In fact, this is a good example of the beginning of a rumination cycle! Here are other versions of this concern: *Why can't I accept the way things are and just be happy? Maybe I'm making a mountain out of a molehill. Other people have it tougher than I do. What if we end up making things worse by trying to make them better?*

The purpose of this book is to help you stop overthinking—not to encourage more of it. When you reflect on different concepts and themes through exercises, journal prompts, or reflections you share with your partner, the type of thinking you'll be doing won't be the same thing as overthinking. Each time you reflect, or think about your thinking, in order to gain a better understanding of cognitive patterns, you're drawing on healthy thinking skills—adaptive self-reflection and metacognition in this case (more on these in chapter 9). Overthinking and rumination, on the other hand, are anxious reactions to triggers.

There's a lot at stake when anxious or unhappy couples maintain the status quo—minimizing, ignoring, or denying the negative impact of overthinking on their love story. To stop ruminating, I'll be inviting you to do some conscious, healthy thinking *about* your overthinking. The more you understand overthinking, the better equipped you'll be to do less of it.

Now that you know the costs and consequences of ignoring overthinking, are you ready to defeat love's quiet enemy? By turning the page, you're answering, "Yes!"

CHAPTER 1

What Is Relationship Rumination?

Ever since William lost his job six weeks ago, the moment he wakes up, a rumination cycle begins. *I can't live on my savings forever,* he worries. *It's impossible to find work at my age. My colleagues probably think I'm a loser. What if I end up homeless and destitute?*

Some days, William is able to cheer himself up, ask friends for help, and research his job options. Most days, though, he lapses into rumination cycles centered on predictable, painful themes. If a job interview goes poorly or colleagues don't respond to his emails fast enough, William ruminates about being unemployable. When he thinks about his past, he recalls his failures and minimizes his successes. His negative thinking undermines his self-confidence. He convinces himself he can't rely on his network or reach out for job leads.

Now let's imagine William in a romantic relationship in the same situation.

I can't live on my savings forever, he worries, listening to the sound of Theo humming in the shower. *My colleagues are probably ignoring my emails on purpose.* William lies in bed staring at the ceiling while Theo—a well-paid graphic designer—gets dressed for work. His rumination pinwheel spins: *What's going to happen to me? Is my career over?* Because he's in a committed relationship, thoughts also arise about his boyfriend. *It's just a matter of time before Theo breaks up with me. He sees me as a burden. I bet he regrets moving in together.*

"Have a good day," Theo calls from the doorway.

"Easy for you to say," William mutters. "*You* have a job."

As Theo drives into the city, he finds himself daydreaming about one of his attractive, successful exes. *Why did I end up moving in with William anyway?* Theo wonders. *He takes everything so seriously. What's the point of living with someone who can't stop worrying all the time?* Without either of them knowing what has happened, William's rumination cycle has touched off a dueling pinwheel in Theo.

General Rumination vs. Relationship Rumination

General rumination is sometimes referred to as negative thinking, worrying, or brooding. In academic circles, it's called negative self-referential processing, or NSRP (Mennin and Fresco 2013). General rumination is probably the kind of rumination you've heard people refer to in casual conversation. It's an unhealthy cognitive style made up of repetitive thoughts rooted mostly in past events. These thoughts center around situations we regret and can't change. General rumination can contribute to depression and anxiety, decrease your motivation, and erode your self-confidence. Although relationship rumination is similar to general rumination, it's also different in important ways—as William's story shows.

Think of general rumination as the equivalent of a bicycle. One person rides it. Relationship rumination, on the other hand, is like a tandem bicycle. You ride general rumination by yourself, but you *both* ride relationship rumination. Tandem bicycles have twice the opportunities for conflicted agendas, backpedaling, and poor weight distribution. On a tandem bicycle, when partners sync their pedaling, the bicycle moves forward smoothly and swiftly. If one partner lurches sideways, though, the results can be disastrous.

And guess what happens if one partner pedals without realizing their chain has fallen off its ring? The other person must pedal twice as hard to keep the bicycle moving. If both chains fall off and partners continue pedaling without getting any traction, it's only a matter of time before the bicycle topples over. This is what happens when partners ruminate.

Just as with general rumination, the more you overthink in your relationship, the more your negative thoughts will influence your mood and behaviors. But relationship rumination doesn't impact you alone. Repetitive, negative thinking pollutes the physical, mental, and emotional space you share with a partner. It leaks out of your mind. This happens in three ways: expressively, through toxic omissions, and energetically.

Expressive Leaks

Even when our thoughts seem hidden, we communicate them in nonverbal ways. They color the ways we express ourselves, whether we mean them to or not. They transmit through our word choices, actions, behaviors, gestures and facial expressions, and how we phrase ideas. They're revealed in the topics we focus on or ignore.

When Lisette sees a mother hugging her toddler on a playground, she's reminded of her own mother, who is undergoing chemotherapy for breast cancer. She also starts thinking about how much she wants a child. When she gets home, she shares this experience with Manuel, tears welling up in her eyes. Manuel gets up and leaves the room, muttering, "I'll get some tissues." One of Lisette's familiar rumination pinwheels starts spinning. *It's pointless to share anything with him. He's not interested. I can't rely on him to listen to me or understand what I need. He probably doesn't even want kids. He's in his own world.* This particular pinwheel makes it hard for Lisette to see how much Manuel actually does care about her.

When he returns with tissues, Lisette avoids eye contact and says flatly, "Thanks."

"Did I do something wrong?" Manuel asks, puzzled.

Lisette shakes her head. "I'm just tired," she says. "I'm going to bed."

Sensitive partners will notice our ruminative thinking more often than less sensitive partners. They pick up on the emotional charge in the words we use when we speak, in our body language when we move, in our facial expressions, and in our behaviors. All partners—even less sensitive ones—will notice it some of the time. Your shared connection taps you into the subtle and not-so-subtle energy shifts created by your thoughts.

Toxic Omission Leaks

Your ruminative thoughts can spread through acts of omission. An act of omission is any time you stifle or withhold your authentic self. When you try to control your partner's reactions and responses in an otherwise healthy relationship by curating or hiding important information, you create toxic omissions.

If you act like you're listening when you're distracted, you're leaking toxic omissions. You're robbing your partner of data they need to make an informed choice about whether or not to continue speaking. You're also leaking toxic omissions when you buy into repetitive, negative thoughts about the need to withhold the truth rather than share something difficult honestly.

Margo meets an attractive colleague for a glass of wine after work without telling her girlfriend Kerri. She rationalizes her choice to keep the meeting a secret. *It's best if Kerri doesn't know everything I do. Privacy isn't the same thing as secrecy. This way she won't get jealous. It's not like I'm having an affair. She'd only blow it out of proportion.*

When Margo arrives home from work, she hugs Kerri, saying, "I'm happy to see you."

"I was expecting you sooner," Kerri murmurs.

"You don't sound very happy to see *me*," Margo teases.

"Of course I am," Kerri says, puzzled by her own sadness.

Energy Leaks

One of the most potent ways our overthinking leaks out of our minds is in the form of energy. We get a vibe we can't explain. There's a contradiction between our partner's words and how they appear, or between what we want to believe and what we sense and observe.

Thoughts manifest in brain waves as a form of electromagnetic energy and therefore have a mass, albeit very small (Das 2020). Is it too far-fetched to suppose that our thoughts—a subtle form of energy—don't vanish completely when we think them? Maybe. But according to the first law of thermodynamics, energy can only be converted, not destroyed. If you've ever rubbed a balloon against your forearm, you've likely noticed an invisible charge raises hair on your skin. What if the energy of your thoughts also transmits in ways seen and unseen, whether through an invisible "charge" or through your tone of voice, facial expressions, movements, and behaviors?

Lisette has turned off the lights and gone to bed. Manuel lies down in the darkness beside her and whispers, "Hey, come here." Although Lisette hasn't said anything else about the mother and the toddler, she's still ruminating about Manuel being unreliable. *He doesn't get me. He's oblivious. He has no idea how upset I am about my mother. His mom is healthy. He really doesn't care about me.* These negative thoughts reinforce her fears and insecurities. When Manuel invites her closer, she tells herself he's only being affectionate out of pity.

Lisette slides across the mattress. Although she wants to kiss and hold Manuel, her cycling thoughts inhibit her. *He probably doesn't find me attractive anymore,* she thinks. *I've gained weight. He wishes I were thinner. I bet he's glad the lights are off.*

Manuel hears Lisette sigh. His momentary desire for intimacy and closeness fades. He feels detached from her. He isn't sure what just happened or why. The vibe isn't right.

SOLO EXERCISE: Relationship Rumination Questionnaire

Use this exercise to increase your awareness of the role rumination plays in your relationship. In a journal, write the numbers 1–30 in a column with each number on its own line. Then read each item listed below and indicate how you would begin each sentence using the numeric scale. Choose the response that corresponds best with what you actually do rather than with what you think you *should* do. To download this questionnaire in PDF format, go to http://www.newharbinger.com/50034.

I never (0), I sometimes (1), I often (2), or I always (3):

1. _____ think I can convince my partner to act a certain way toward me.

2. _____ think, *They may leave me if I don't find a way to make them stay.*

3. _____ think, *I should end this now since I'm going to disappoint my partner.*

4. _____ think of all the ways I could have handled past events better as a partner.

5. _____ think, *If I were better at relationships, I wouldn't suffer.*

6. _____ think, *Everyone else is in a better place than I am with my partner.*

7. _____ analyze my partner's actions, words, and behaviors.

8. _____ analyze myself, my actions, my words, and my behaviors in relationship.

9. _____ keep most of my thoughts from my partner because they're too negative.

10. _____ think about painful subjects without sharing my thoughts with my partner.

11. _____ think, *My partner is too negative, and they should be more positive.*

12. _____ overshare in the hopes it'll bring us closer, then second-guess what or how much I've shared.

13. _____ think other couples are happier than us.

14. _____ spend a lot of time deciphering my partner's intentions.

15. _____ spend a lot of time deciphering my own wants.

16. _____ fantasize about going someplace alone where I'll forget about my relationship.

17. _____ fantasize about becoming more attractive or successful·so my partner will love me more.

18. _____ spend a lot of time comparing us with a better past relationship.

19. _____ imagine sad future scenarios with my partner based on sad past scenarios.

20. _____ think, *There's something wrong with how I think about us.*

21. _____ think, *It's unfair that our relationship is so challenging.*

22. _____ think, *I should be happier than I am with my partner.*

23. _____ think, *They should be happier with me.*

24. _____ think, *Something's wrong with me as a partner.*

25. _____ think, *Something's wrong with them as a partner.*

26. _____ think, *I can't function in this partnership.*

27. _____ think, *We've been through bad times, and they're going to happen again.*

28. _____ get mad at myself for bringing us down.

29. _____ get mad at my partner for bringing us down.

30. _____ think, *I can't stand how much stress my/their overthinking causes me.*

A lot of 2s and 3s suggests more overthinking. Mostly 0s and 1s suggests less. While you may be closer to perceiving the different forms relationship rumination can take after doing this exercise, it can still be challenging to spot it, when it's happening—especially in the moment.

Why It's Hard to Spot

In therapy, one of the first things I ask couples to do is identify their problem. *What* a couple identifies as their problem influences the strategies they use to resolve it. When something isn't working, you need to discover what's wrong before seeking solutions.

If you hire a general contractor to fix a yellow stain on a ceiling, they'll look into what created it before applying a fresh coat of paint. When there's a stain on a ceiling, the problem appears to be external. The stain looks ugly. But because there could be a leaky pipe in the walls, the contractor doesn't immediately apply a fresh coat of paint and hope for the best. Instead, they consider how the stain got there. Did a pipe burst? Is rainwater trickling into the walls? Does the house need a new roof? Did something go wrong with a duct or a vent? They look for a root cause. If the contractor dismisses or ignores a ceiling stain, or paints over it when it resurfaces, they're setting the customer up for a much bigger problem in the future (Shapiro 2019).

In the same way, the external problem you perceive in your relationship may be a symptom of internal causes. You may identify your problem as communication issues because your partner arrives late even when they agreed to arrive on time. When you point this out, they may get defensive, accusing you of making a big deal over nothing. But this so-called communication problem may not be about your surface-level agreements. Your problem as a couple may be less about the words you speak and more about unspoken assumptions, expectations, feelings, needs, and fears you're not openly discussing.

Going below the surface can be hard to do. It means surrendering to a process you don't fully control and can't predict. It requires a willingness to open yourself to uncomfortable discoveries. Surrendering and opening to the unknown are vulnerable experiences. For most of us, it's never easy to venture into strange territory where dark, forgotten, or disagreeable specters may lurk. Especially if we're anxious or experiencing stress, we may define our problems in simplistic ways that comfort us with the promise of quick, easy solutions.

Fear of the unknown—and a desire for comfort and relief—mislead us into adopting premature "solutions" to relationship problems. We focus on the words we speak and on our partner's words or revisit agreements that were made and broken. We misidentify the problem as poor communication or a lack of timeliness, a character flaw in ourselves or our partner, or a past mistake our partner made that we can't forgive. We convince ourselves that everything would be fine if our partner could just say the right things in the right ways.

But when you ignore or minimize internal causes and contributors to relationship problems—thoughts, assumptions, expectations, feelings, needs, and fears—your solutions don't stick. This is because you're doing the equivalent of painting over the ceiling stain without addressing the cracked pipes or faulty roof. If you and your partner have found yourselves struggling to fix a tricky couples' problem that keeps cropping up over and over again despite your efforts to resolve it, a hidden cause may be relationship rumination. The next sections explain four of the biggest reasons why relationship rumination is hard to recognize—and offer some tips on what you can do to spot it more often.

Defenses Are Invisible

Across therapy models—whether the focus is on thoughts or emotions—rumination operates as a defense. Defenses are mental or behavioral coping strategies used to avoid some other experience. They're like red herrings in mystery novels. Red herrings are misleading or distracting clues that divert the reader's attention away from the main event or focus.

Ruminative thoughts distract you from your own vulnerability. If you don't take the time or make the effort to recognize your defenses, you probably won't see them. Unexamined defenses masquerade as a fixed, permanent part of who you are—like your height or eye color. When you choose to pay attention to the defenses you use, you can begin to see them more clearly. They're clues to the vulnerability that's hidden by your overthinking.

Let's say your girlfriend hasn't responded to a text you sent her six hours ago. You're upset, and you think, *What's she doing? Has she forgotten about me? Is she ghosting me on purpose? I thought she enjoyed our weekend as much as I did. Is she already tired of me?* You do this without even knowing how you feel about her delayed response to your text.

Repetitive negative thinking kicks in as a defense against your own emotions. As you tell a friend about your weekend with your girlfriend, you focus on all the ways she disappointed you.

"Do you miss her?" your friend asks suddenly. The question unsettles you—but only for a split second. You quickly suppress the uncomfortable emotions you'd prefer not to feel.

"Hell no!" you laugh. "I'm better off alone. I'm not ready to settle down."

But what if you answered your friend's question differently?

Exhaling and letting yourself feel what's under the fog of negative thoughts, imagine responding to your friend's question like this: "You know, I *do* miss her."

Your friend nods. You're confirming something they sensed.

"Maybe that's why I'm focusing on all the bad stuff right now," you might continue. "I hate to admit it, but I feel lonely without her. It's not a good feeling."

When you let yourself feel what you actually feel—however uncomfortable it is to do this—you open to a new possibility. Your overthinking about your girlfriend is a protection against heartache and longing. Because you can see it and feel it, your repetitive negative thoughts don't become the lens through which you view her and deny what's true for you.

Rumination Is Overlooked as a Couples' Problem

Most people don't know what they're looking at when it comes to the "ceiling stains" caused by repetitive, negative thinking. Even couples therapists seldom talk about relationship rumination as a couple's *shared* problem. If overthinking is mentioned at all, it's the problem of one person—the ruminator. This is because negative thinking, distorted thinking, and rumination are viewed as strings of reflexive thoughts in a single person's mind, the ruminator's responsibility, not a relationship issue—right?

Wrong.

Take Eddie and Chandra. Neither of them is certain where they'll live after they graduate with nursing degrees from the West Coast university where they met. Every time Chandra tells Eddie she loves him, he starts overthinking. *What does she want from me? Does she think I'll agree to move to Chicago? She's probably trying to lure me in. I bet she wouldn't say she loved me if she knew how scared I am. It's only a matter of time before I let her down.*

Eddie regularly dismisses Chandra's expressions of affection toward him. He jokes about dating a walking Hallmark card. As a result, Chandra stops expressing her affection. *I guess I shouldn't be so open with him,* she thinks. *Maybe he doesn't believe me. Or maybe he's not as serious about us as I am.* When Chandra stops saying "I love you," it triggers more of Eddie's overthinking: *I knew she didn't mean it. It's only a matter of time before people leave you behind. This is why it's better not to trust anyone.*

If you looked at Eddie's rumination as solely his issue, distinct from his relationship with Chandra, you might say he had trust issues or feared commitment. If you looked at Chandra's rumination separately from her relationship with Eddie, you might conclude she had low self-esteem and couldn't speak up and share more honestly. But even if Eddie does have trust issues and even if Chandra does struggle with self-esteem and speaking up, it's the way they're ruminating that fuels their problems as a couple.

You would probably agree with me when I say that your thoughts influence your words, actions, and body language. What you may not be as aware of is how your rumination impacts both you and your partner. Once you frame relationship rumination as a couple's shared problem, it's no longer about blaming one person or pointing fingers. You become allies, regardless of who happens to be overthinking from one day to the next.

It's Thinking, Not Behavior

Thoughts aren't visible. We can't observe them in the same ways we observe physical objects or events unfolding in the external world. We can't taste them, hear them, smell them, or touch them. They're harder to perceive. Most of the time, when we think something, we get caught up in the flow of thoughts in our minds as if these thoughts were reality rather than thoughts *about* reality. We regularly merge ourselves with our thinking and mistake our thoughts for absolute truth. In cognitive behavioral therapy, this phenomenon has a name: cognitive fusion.

Cognitive fusion makes rumination hard to spot because we're so invested in believing our thoughts that we don't recognize that they are actually interpretations. If we know our thoughts aren't accurate representations of reality just because we happen to think them, we can check them for accuracy before believing them. We can consider alternative thoughts that might be as true as the ones we're having—or more true. This can help us protect our relationship from the barrage of falsehoods our minds reflexively create with repetitive, negative thinking.

One way to begin spotting rumination is to make a distinction between two different types of thinking: active and passive. Active, directed thinking is rarely ruminative thinking. Passive, automatic thinking, on the other hand, is rumination's bread and butter.

Active thinking emerges from a conscious choice to address a problem, follow an intention, create something, or understand an issue more deeply. It involves will and attention. You have a desire to achieve a goal, and you harness your cognitive powers to help you do it. The sequences of thoughts that have led you to seek out this book are examples of active thinking. You want to improve your relationship and reduce rumination, so you think actively about different options and take steps to move toward your goal.

Passive thinking, on the other hand, runs on its own. It's there whether you're aware of it or not. It hisses along like a natural gas leak. Sometimes, passive thinking is there in reactive, mixed-up chatter that makes it hard for you to reap the benefits of the positive steps you take. Sometimes it's there in a fog of images, vague emotions, and stories. Right now, as you're reading, there may be passive thoughts in the background of your mind that you're barely conscious of. *Is reading a book like this going to make a difference? What if I change and my partner doesn't? I'm not sure I can wait much longer for things to improve.*

Relationship rumination is passive thinking. Passive thoughts cycle through your mind while your attention remains scattered or externally focused. For example, your partner may ask, "How come we don't spend any time together?" A third of your attention may be on their rigid posture and tense facial expression; a third on their tone of voice and words; and a third on flipping through a takeout menu while figuring out what to order for dinner.

You might have little or no awareness of the passive thoughts spinning in your mind, triggered by your partner's words. Nonetheless, these thoughts are there, quietly influencing the situation: *What did I do wrong now? How come they're always unhappy with me? Why can't they just let things be without complaining?* Your passive thoughts will shape how you speak and act with your partner.

We Think It's Helpful

Steeping in so many thinking messages over decades can turn thinking into our automatic response to life. Because it's the air we breathe, we don't question it as an effective coping strategy.

Many people mistake overthinking as helpful because some thinking styles *can* be helpful. Thinking strategies such as adaptive self-reflection, problem solving, and positive reappraisal (more on these in chapter 9) help us overcome challenges and work through problems. But when healthy thinking gets derailed by overthinking and becomes rumination, it can be hard to tell the difference between helpful and unhelpful thinking styles. Learning from difficult or painful experiences by reviewing them in your mind is an important skill. So is assessing future possibilities. But getting depressed because you can't stop reliving the past hurts you. So does raising your stress level by imagining how much could go wrong in the future.

Many people convince themselves that the repetitive, negative messages in their rumination cycles motivate them to accomplish important things. I've heard this from clients who live inside minds where an incessant stream of self-judgment and self-blame push them to "get things right" and "be better." Compassionate forms of personal motivation may be foreign to you if family members or other influential people have convinced you that worry and self-criticism are acceptable ways of improving yourself and overcoming hardships.

But the truth is, people succeed in life and love *in spite* of rumination, not because of it.

So then, if rumination *isn't* helpful, why do we do it?

The Threat Link

When we ruminate, it's usually because we feel threatened by something. Our mind associates some internal or external event, person, or situation with danger. I call this danger association *the threat link*. The threat link operates unconsciously, and it's what activates our triggers. Triggers are particular kinds of sensory input—images, sounds, words, smells, events, situations, or people—that feel threatening because of what you unconsciously associate with them. Usually, triggers cause you to react emotionally, which distorts your understanding of what's actually happening (we'll explore triggers in more depth in chapter 5). The threat link does this by connecting an internal or external event with forgotten, dismissed, or otherwise unwanted internal experiences. Put another way, the threat link creates our triggers by linking a person, experience, or event with one (or more) of our vulnerabilities.

A simple equation illustrating how this works might look like this:

internal/external event + activated threat link = trigger

Triggers can be sensations, objects, or events (Pittman and Karle 2015). Frequently, once a threat is activated, it sets off rumination cycles. Both a sharp pain in your back and driving by a hospital can activate a threat link and set off a cycle of ruminative thoughts. *What if my husband gets sick? How will I survive if something happens to him? I can't even put gas in my car without his help. I wish I were more independent. God, I'm pathetic.*

Eating strawberries can also activate a threat link and set off a similarly grim sequence of thoughts. *Oh, no, I forgot to wash off these strawberries before eating them! They cover them with pesticides. How could I be so stupid? What if eating them ends up making me sick?*

Threat links are personal and subjective. They highlight dangers you associate with a sensation, object, person, experience, or event. When a trigger links with something that evokes threat in your mind, two clusters of nuclei in the brain called the amygdalae (referred to in this book as "amygdala," the term most commonly used for them) sound an alarm. The amygdala signals danger to other brain structures connected with your autonomic nervous system. This happens pretty much instantly.

The amygdala keeps things simple: you're either safe or you're in danger. It receives sensory input from other parts of the brain. It communicates with the sympathetic and parasympathetic nervous systems by attaching a code-red message to stimuli it has learned to consider dangerous. This message is then sent to the brain's motor systems and the hippocampus. "(A)t times of extreme fear," Robert Sapolsky (2017) writes in *Behave: The Biology of Humans at Our Best and Worst,* "the amygdala pulls the hippocampus into a type of fear learning" (42).

Your amygdala doesn't understand time, the difference between reality and imagination, or gradations in intensity, degree, or probability. It registers danger when there's a close enough fit between a current trigger and what has been threatening in the past. To the amygdala, a close-enough fit doesn't have to be all that close. It errs on the side of caution.

How does the threat link function in romantic relationships?

Imagine sitting at a table in a coffee shop on a sunny Saturday morning with your partner. A waitress cheerfully takes your order. After she walks away, your partner leans toward you and whispers, "Don't you think she looks like Gal Gadot?" The amygdala connects this comment to past experiences that have led you to feel insecure about your attractiveness, attaching a code-red signal to your partner's comment. Before you're aware of the trigger, your amygdala sets off a chain reaction of protective and defensive responses (Pittman and Karle 2015). Your heart rate speeds up, and your blood pressure increases. Neurochemicals spill into your bloodstream.

The same information setting off your amygdala arrives at your cortex too, milliseconds later. By the time your rational mind catches up with what's happening inside you, your body has prepped itself to fight, freeze, or flee. This is the point at which rumination kicks in. Sensing the body's anxiety, your cortex uses its cognitive abilities to control, manage, and make sense of a formless internal experience of danger. How does your mind exert control? Take a wild guess.

Bingo. Overthinking.

Unfortunately, once the amygdala has tagged something as dangerous, it's hard to be objective in the moment. Your threat link is buzzing. You perceive things around you through a rolling fog of fear. Suddenly, the cheerful waitress who took your order looks smug and mean, as if she knows she could steal your partner away from you with a wink and a smile. Your mind spins thoughts like, *Why is he looking at the freaking waitress? This is supposed to be our special time together. How dare he leer at other women. I should just get up and leave. He doesn't even care that we're in public. It's humiliating. He doesn't respect me!*

When you're in a low-grade state of anxiety, the sense of being under threat impacts your mood, nervous system, circulation, breathing, and muscle tone. If your partner's face is neutral as he leans across the table, you won't perceive it as neutral anymore once your amygdala has flagged his comment about the waitress with a code-red signal. From that point on, you're primed to misperceive his facial expression as hostile, mocking, or indifferent.

Groundbreaking discoveries in molecular biology have shown how messages transmitted by our thoughts shape us on a cellular level (Lipton 2015). Modern medicine and new imaging technologies have given scientists and researchers a window into how our thoughts affect our bodies and brains. When you believe you're under threat, the sympathetic nervous system gets mobilized. Your middle-ear regulation shifts to lower and higher tones. These are the tones of predation and distress (Dana

2018). In other words, when you feel threatened, you're more likely to perceive the world around you as threatening—even when it's not.

Now imagine that instead of the Gal Gadot comment, your partner whispers, "You're beautiful." What a sweet thing to say—right? What could be dangerous about a compliment? Except that you grew up with a moralistic parent who insisted bad people focus on physical attractiveness. In that case, your amygdala might register a well-intentioned compliment as a threat. Before you realize it, the amygdala's code-red signal lights up, you experience your partner's comment as a trigger, and a subtle fight, flight, or freeze response kicks in. You may cope with your discomfort by ruminating about your partner's words and intentions. *Is he being sincere? What if he's manipulating me? Or what if he only loves me now for how I look and not for who I am? What if one day he decides I'm not beautiful anymore? Will he bail?*

In this case, the threat link runs through uncomfortable memories, longings, impulses, dreams, and regrets connected to your moralistic parent and how they raised you to view your own physical attractiveness. You may ruminate without realizing your amygdala has linked your partner's compliment to your past in a way that feels threatening.

Most of us are pretty good at recognizing dramatic forms of fight, flight, and freeze. We're familiar with the fight reactions of yelling and punching or the crouched posture of a soldier avoiding detection. In a common flight reaction, movie heroes throw themselves out of trains, cars, or buses to escape villains. But what about when we come home late from a concert and our partner's shoulders slump? Or the impulse to start cleaning out the kitchen junk drawer when our partner mentions their biological clock ticking? Or the numbness we feel in response to our partner's excitement about winning an award? Or the tension in our partner's jaw when we playfully mention a sexual fantasy we'd like to test out?

Although these fight, flight, and freeze reactions aren't as obvious or dramatic as punching, jumping out of cars, and assuming a stonelike posture, they're still signs of an active threat link. It's worth it to get curious about them. If you don't know why your amygdala attaches a code-red signal to something your partner says or does, ask yourself, "Am I feeling a little bit threatened right now?"

SOLO EXERCISE: Getting Grounded in One Breath

One way to shift the amygdala's code-red signal to code yellow is through relaxation. Relaxation can start with focusing on one breath—the breath you're taking right now. Starting with one breath keeps this practice simple and easy to remember. As long as you're alive, you're always breathing, so there's always a breath to work with.

Whether you get grounded in one, three, or fifty consecutive breaths, you're focusing on the breath you're taking in the here and now. Getting grounded doesn't happen in the breath you just took, or in the one that's about to come. It's happening while you read this sentence. The only breath you can ever take happens in the present.

Don't worry about doing this practice "right." Attending closely to a single breath, from beginning to end, can be the first small step you take toward getting grounded in your body and in the present moment when something triggers you or you become aware that you're ruminating. You can find an audio recording of this practice at http://www.newharbinger .com/50034.

Begin by closing your eyes and breathing through your nose. Without changing anything about the way you breathe, observe the air flowing in and out of your nostrils. Pay attention to one inhale from the microsecond when it starts to when it ends. Take in, as fully as possible, the physical sensations that go with this inhale. Some sensations you may notice are:

* a hint of warmth or coolness along the rims of your nostrils

* a slight tingling in your nasal cavities

* a subtle expansion of your lungs

* your ribs lifting and spreading

* a micro-moment at the top of the inhale when no air moves.

Now, pay attention to the exhale that follows this inhale. If you've gotten distracted or lost your focus, don't worry. Pay attention to the next exhale you're able to focus on. Be with the physical experience of the exhale from its starting point to its end point. Allow the experience to unfold effortlessly. Some sensations you may notice are:

* above your lip, the light touch of air leaving your body through your nostrils

* a subtle contraction of muscles in your chest

* a settling sensation across your shoulders

* a micro-moment at the bottom of the exhale when no air moves.

Short-Term Benefits of Rumination

If there were no benefits to rumination, we wouldn't do it. First, it temporarily reduces anxiety. Second, it gives us an illusion of control. Third, it's familiar.

Because none of us want to experience discomfort, we try to escape it. As we've seen, an easy and socially sanctioned way of escaping discomfort is through overthinking. If our minds can't control an uncomfortable situation, but we also don't want to be with it, we ruminate.

Let's take a closer look at each of these short-term benefits. This way, you'll know what false comforts you'll be giving up when you interrupt your overthinking.

It Reduces Anxiety

The word *rumination* comes from the Latin word *ruminatus*, which means "to chew the cud" or "turn (something) over in the mind" (Webster's New World College Dictionary, 5th ed., 2018, s.v. "rumination"). Cud is what's created when a cow goes through at least one round of chewing and swallows their feed into a section of their stomachs called the rumen. But when cows chew cud, they're relaxed, healthy, and comfortable, and they produce more and better milk. When you engage in rumination—the human, mental version of cud-chewing—you're far from relaxed and comfortable. Most of the time, you're anxious. Rumination is a double-edged sword. It temporarily reduces anxiety while also fueling it.

It's the night before Darlene and Michael's engagement dinner. Darlene's father is an outspoken democrat, and Michael's father is a passionate republican. Their fathers have met once before, and when the conversation turned to politics, it was a disaster. Darlene starts to worry about what will happen. The more anxious she becomes, the more she ruminates, and the more she ruminates, the more anxious she becomes. Her anxiety peaks when she hears Michael talking to his father in the next room in a low voice, asking him not to drink at the dinner. She soothes herself by making a beeline to the freezer and eating two pints of ice cream.

Most of us have engaged in well-intentioned self-sabotage like this. It's a tragic human foible. As Darlene works her way through the ice cream, she forgets her concerns about the upcoming dinner, outspoken fathers, and politics. Soon afterward though, her anxious overthinking returns; only now, she feel ashamed *and* sick. *Why did I do that? Will I be able to sleep? God, that was dumb. Will I still fit into my engagement outfit?* Eating ice cream brought Darlene short-term satisfaction followed by long-term negative consequences. Her coping strategy made the problem worse.

Like eating too much ice cream, overthinking brings temporary relief at a high cost. Doing it *sometimes* probably won't hurt your relationship much. But doing it a lot can hurt your relationship a lot. In contrast to cud-chewing in our bovine friends, rumination won't lead you to a longer, more productive life or happier relationship. Quite the opposite. Rather than helping you digest your mental feed, it makes the problem you can't stomach even more indigestible.

It Gives the Illusion of Control

In a study titled "Neurobiological Substrates of Dread," researchers at Emory University School of Medicine studied the brain activity of volunteer subjects who waited to receive a shock for an unknown time period (Berns et al. 2006). The study showed that given the choice between a stronger and a weaker shock, many people will choose a stronger shock administered earlier over waiting for a weaker shock that will arrive at some unspecified moment in the future. Ruminating functions in a similar way. We engage in it even though it hurts us. When we ruminate, we're attempting to stay in control, even if letting go of control would be less painful. Like the subjects in the "dread" study who couldn't stand knowing an unpleasant event might happen at some unknown point in the future, we choose the more painful *zing* of repetitive, negative thinking to the unsettling experience of uncertainty.

It's Familiar

From a very young age, we've received hundreds—even thousands—of messages about how *thinking* is superior to *being*. We've come to believe thinking is for adults, being is for children. Thinking is strong, being is weak. Thinking is useful, being is unproductive. These messages reinforce our view of thinking as the best and most familiar, go-to solution. Because certain kinds of thinking *are* helpful, we may believe *all* thinking helps us cope.

Familiarity is easily mistaken for safety. But familiarity and safety aren't the same thing. Sometimes, doing what's familiar has disastrous consequences. In business, if you invest in companies you're familiar with because you shop at their stores, own their devices, or use their products, you risk overinvesting in companies you're familiar with rather than creating a diversified portfolio that can weather the ups and downs of a changing market. People with little experience flying insist they're safer in a car than in a plane, but a 2017 article in *Fortune* magazine analyzed data from the National Highway Safety Travel Administration and the National Safety Transportation Board and concluded that Americans have a 1 in 114 chance of dying in a car accident as compared to 1 in 9,821 in a plane crash (Jenkins 2017). As you expand your definition of safety beyond what's familiar, prepare to get a little uncomfortable.

JOINT EXERCISE: What Rumination Does for Me

Find a quiet place to sit without distractions. Use the "Getting Grounded in One Breath" exercise to center yourself or listen to the audio recording at http://www.newharbinger.com/50034.

Bring to mind a recent situation when you were caught in a cycle of over-thinking. Rather than thinking *about* it or rehashing different details of what happened, mentally step back from the situation as you recall it. Observe it as if it were a miniature diorama in a snow globe.

Write your responses to the questions below in a journal. If you want to, share your answers with your partner (refer to the Speaker and Listener responsibilities for a refresher on creating safety and supporting connection as you speak and listen).

* What might your overthinking have done for you in this situation?

* Was it a familiar habit you fell into?

* Did it reduce your anxiety, at least temporarily, distracting you from something uncomfortable?

* Did it give you an illusion of control?

* Did it feed some aspect of your identity you're attached to— such as being right, looking good, or being the one who is always at fault?

* If so, could you relax your grip on this aspect of your identity by reminding yourself, "I don't have to be right," "I don't have to look good," or "I'm not always at fault"?

JOINT EXERCISE: My Blocks to Spotting Overthinking

Select one high-scoring item from the "Relationship Rumination Questionnaire" you completed earlier in this chapter. If you haven't com-pleted it, glance through it and choose an item you know you do a lot. What gets in the way of noticing the negative thoughts represented by this item?

Do they hum along in the background, outside of your conscious awareness? Do you believe the thinking represented by this item is helpful in some way? Does thinking like this temporarily reduce your anxiety?

In the Speaker and Listener roles, share with one another a technique or practice that might help you bring awareness to this item in the future. For example, if you circled item number twenty-seven ("I often think we've been through tough times and they're bound to happen again"), you might tell your partner, "I don't realize it's harmful when I think this way. I actually think I'm doing a good thing by bracing myself for the worst."

In terms of one thing you've learned so far that might help you bring awareness to these thoughts, you might say, "I'll practice getting grounded in one breath," or "I'll remind myself of some of the 'being messages' from the 'Being and Thinking Messages Checklist' exercise."

To download a PDF worksheet of this exercise, go to http://www.newhar binger.com/50034.

Rumination Cycles

Like the Spinning Beachball of Death or a snowball rolling downhill and gathering momentum, ruminative thoughts turn in a seemingly endless loop around the same painful themes. I've identified five distinct rumination cycles centered on the themes of blame, control, doubt, worry, and self-pity. Their similarities and differences are listed here:

- Blame, doubt, and self-pity cycles are past-oriented.

- Worry and control cycles are future-oriented.

- Blame, doubt, and worry cycles target either a partner, oneself, or both.

- Self-pity cycles are focused on oneself as a victim.

Each rumination cycle points toward a shortage of some important psychological nutrient. When you recognize a rumination cycle, you can bring this nutrient in as an antidote—a particular focus or approach that will help counteract this cycle. I'll discuss each cycle in detail, along with their antidotes, in the sections that follow. Here's an overview of psychological nutrients you can draw on to slow or stop each rumination cycle before it snowballs:

- If blame cycles are your go-to form of overthinking, practice acceptance.

- If you find yourself worrying a lot, connect with your body in the here and now.

- If doubt is your main form of relationship rumination, expand your ability to trust.

- If you spin control cycles, let go of perfectionism and what's outside of your control.

- If you spin self-pity cycles, take responsibility for your contribution to problems.

All of us are capable of spinning all the rumination cycles, and it's not unusual to spin a hybrid of two or even three of them at once. But most of us have a dominant cycle: the one we spin most often. We may spin it so much that it colors our identity and personality. As you investigate your own dominant rumination cycle, you'll probably discover you have a secondary one too. This is the cycle you spin when your dominant cycle fails to bring resolution, relief, or closure.

As you identify your dominant and secondary cycles, get curious about what triggers them. Draw on practices that can help you counteract your cycle's reality-distorting power by cultivating the missing "nutrient" of acceptance, being present in your body, trust, letting go of perfectionism and control, and taking responsibility for your contribution to problems.

Blame Cycle. Antidote: Practice Acceptance

This is my fault. I'm such an idiot. How could I let this happen? It's unacceptable, intolerable, horrible, awful. My partner is selfish. They're wrong.

They should pay for this. They should apologize. Don't they realize how much pain they're causing me?

Thoughts, memories, and images in the blame cycle revolve around painful past events. A conversation escalated into a fight. You're sure you've been unfairly treated, taken advantage of, and misunderstood. You had good intentions, and your partner misinterpreted what you said or did. You planned a special trip, and your partner ruined it with their irritability. The dinner ended awkwardly for you and your dinner guests. You recall the past selectively. Events confirming your own (or your partner's) flaws are magnified.

Has your partner ever sincerely praised you for something you reflexively denied or minimized? Maybe they said, "You look great," and you responded, "No, I don't," or "I'm tired." Maybe they said, "It was so thoughtful of you to pick me up from the airport," and you said, "Well, of course, why wouldn't I?" When you spin blame cycles, you're too busy blaming your partner—or yourself—to take love in.

When blame is directed at your partner, it's fueled by aggression and resentment. As long as you focus on what's wrong with your partner, you don't have to look at your contribution to problems. You can cry, "I'm innocent!" A false sense of superiority protects you from the truth of your own human imperfections and flaws. When you direct it at yourself, it's sustained by guilt, shame, and regret. You're self-critical. You should have known better.

If blame cycles are your go-to form of overthinking, you suffer from an acceptance shortage. Practice accepting what you normally blame yourself or your partner for. If you blame your partner for regularly taking the last sheet of toilet paper on the roll without putting in a replacement roll, accept the fact that they do this (you may as well since they're doing it whether you accept it or not). If you blame your partner for their current stress level, try accepting it instead. They *are* under stress right now. It *is* happening. If you blame yourself for being angry, accept your anger. How does it help you or anyone else for you to reject what you already are?

.You don't have to *like* something to accept it. You don't have to give up on expressing your needs and wishes either or on improving your life and your relationship. You can accept your partner taking the last sheet of toilet paper without putting in a new roll, and at the same time, you can let your partner know how you feel and what you want when you're calm and they're more likely to hear your feedback. You can say, "When you take the last sheet of toilet paper without putting in a new roll, I get mad. It puts me in a tough position. Can you replace the roll next time?" Doing this with acceptance increases the chances of your partner listening and altering their behavior since the negative charge of blame isn't leaking into the relationship field, raising their defenses, and making it harder for them to relate to you.

Control Cycle. Antidote: Release Perfectionism and What You Can't Control

I know best. I'm rational. I'm in touch with my emotions. My views should hold sway. I'm more genuine. I'm kinder, wiser, healthier, superior, younger, older. Because I'm the extravert, I'm more suited to organize our social life. I'm the one who keeps us healthy, safe, and happy. I'm justified in pursuing and enforcing my agenda. I'm the one who knows how to handle this.

These thoughts orbit a desired future outcome and the best way to achieve it. Your partner must sit down at the table immediately. They must talk to someone—a therapist, parent, boss, or realtor—ASAP. It's time for an emergency meeting with your attorney because you know what the next step is. You're curious about consensual nonmonogamy, and so they should be too. It's time to go to Hawaii. You're done with long-distance relationships. You're showing up on your partner's doorstep with a suitcase, a toothbrush, and an espresso machine.

Tension, mistrust, and inflexibility accompany the control cycle. Thoughts have a moralistic edge. You believe in externally defined truths—and you're the one who knows what they are. Your partner *should* and *must* fulfill your vision of the relationship. Possibilities and options are black-and-white. There's good or bad, right or wrong, healthy or unhealthy.

Although you may generally be loyal and thoughtful, in this cycle, your interactions are strategic. Different opinions are unacceptable. You're invested in one outcome—yours.

If you're in the control cycle a lot, get grounded in one breath often. Remind yourself that absolute certainty and invulnerability are pipe dreams. You *can* relax control over others and life wisely and gradually. You can entertain a more complex, nuanced worldview. Practice enjoying the process of whatever it is that you're doing instead of striving for a predetermined or "perfect" outcome. What if events *can* unfold in everyone's best interests even when you don't micromanage them? Ask yourself, "Is this person, event or situation mine to control? Will control get me what I truly want here?"

Doubt Cycle. Antidote: Cultivate Trust

Can I be sure of my own perceptions? Maybe I'm imagining things. Did what I think took place really happen? Why is every other couple doing better than we are? Why did I choose my partner? Is there someone smarter, kinder, more attractive, or richer out there for me? Why did my partner choose me? Am I a fraud? Can I trust my own choices? My intuition has misled me in the past. What if I keep making poor choices?

Gaslighting refers to a form of psychological manipulation done by one person to another where the gaslighter disorients the gaslightee by denying, minimizing, questioning, and undermining their perceptions of reality. In this cycle, your own overthinking gaslights *you*. You selectively recall, minimize, and deny what you know. Or else you overdramatize embarrassing, shameful, or negative aspects of things you've done and choices you've made. Like a fisherman casting a line into a stagnant pond, these kinds of thoughts fly and land with a plop. They don't hook what they're trying to catch. There's never enough certainty. There are never absolute guarantees. No evidence is ever ironclad enough to support your choices, decisions, or actions. Good times seem insubstantial and fleeting. Searching for evidence only reinforces doubts.

Painful insecurity and self-judgment are the hallmarks of chronic doubt cycles. The more you overthink, the less you trust your own recollections and intuition. You risk giving others' negative perceptions of you—real or imagined—more importance than they deserve.

When your overthinking regularly gaslights you, caring feedback from a supportive partner can open your eyes to a broader perspective. It can reduce the imbalance created by your constant second-guessing of yourself and your choices. If the thoughts in your doubt cycles undermine your own or your partner's assessment of your strengths, accomplishments, and positive qualities, recognize it. Remind yourself, "Here's doubt, gaslighting me again."

Invest yourself fully in the process of living your life even when your choices don't deliver the results you expect on your timeline. Make decisions and choices to the best of your ability even when the outcome can't be known in advance. Be gentle with yourself and cultivate realistic expectations. When things don't work out the way you want them to, *be with* the vulnerability you feel instead of *thinking about* how you shouldn't have trusted yourself. Remind yourself, "I'm doing the best I can with the knowledge and abilities I have. Missing the mark and learning is part of being human and relating authentically to other people."

Worry Cycle. Antidote: Connect with Your Body in the Here and Now

What will happen if he gets hurt on the job? What if we divorce and I don't see our children as much as I do now? What if they stop loving me? She might cancel our next date if she finds out I'm a type-1 diabetic. One of us might catch Covid and give it to my father. This could be the last time we're happy together as a couple.

Ruminative worry is an attempt to generate knowledge through forecasting and prediction. But nobody can truly know what will happen in advance. In this cycle, positive outcomes are dismissed or ignored. Worst-case scenarios rule. Fear keeps this cycle going.

You convince yourself you'll be safe as long as you prepare for the worst. Your mind does this by thinking of everything that could go wrong. Instead of helping you feel safer, this strategy heightens your sensitivity to danger. Like a game of psychological whack-a-mole, for every worst-case scenario you think of and imagine fixing, another worst-case scenario pops up. There's no way you can prepare for every potential catastrophe or possible negative outcome.

If you spin worry cycles regularly, the antidote is connecting with your body in the here and now. Worry commandeers awareness, siphoning it away from the present moment and wasting it on a nonexistent future. Tuning into your body can bring your awareness back to what *does* exist: You. Now. Use the "Getting Grounded in One Breath" exercise or listen to the audio at http://www.newharbinger.com/50034 to practice being in your body with this one breath you're taking. Like oil and water, worry and the present moment don't mix.

When you find yourself worrying about an event or situation, insight meditation teacher and founder of Mindful Shenandoah Valley Shell Fischer has a mantra she offers retreatants. She suggests settling in, getting grounded in your body, and then saying these words to yourself as often as you need to: "If this thing I fear transpires the way I would like it to, that would be great. If it doesn't, that will be okay, too, because either way, I am and will be okay."

Self-Pity Cycle. Antidote: Take Responsibility for Your Part

Why me? There's nothing I can do. Life is unfair. I don't deserve this. How come bad things always happen to me? I've tried everything. My situation is hopeless. We don't stand a chance as a couple. Nothing makes a difference. The universe is against me. Suffering is my destiny. There's no solution. Giving up is my only option. Nothing will ever change.

The self-pity cycle kicks in when the other cycles don't bring resolution or relief. If you convince yourself you're never the problem or are always wrongly treated, you can ignore your own irresponsibility, selfishness, immaturity, or passivity. Self-pity distracts you from your part in creating or sustaining hurtful situations. Life looks simple through a fairy-tale lens of good and bad, right and wrong, particularly if you're always on the "right" side of the lens. Often, the unacknowledged expectation is that by embracing the role of a victim, you'll inspire your partner to rescue you. But when you make your partner responsible for your wellbeing or behave as though you're completely helpless when you're not, they end up feeling controlled.

Even if your partner bends over backward to help you feel better, sooner or later, they will get annoyed with you. They may complain of feeling manipulated. When you use self-pity to extract care or concern, you take advantage of other people's goodness.

Often, the self-pity cycle is a reaction to unacknowledged shame, self-judgment, and self-hatred. It's a weak substitute for the self-acceptance and self-love a person caught in self-pity truly longs for. People who find themselves spinning self-pity cycles can work on grieving losses, changing or accepting a difficult situation, and taking responsibility for their part in creating relationship problems. Forgive yourself for things you've said or done reactively or defensively. Allow yourself to feel remorse and make amends for what you've done. If you face your flaws, it brings you closer to self-acceptance than denying them or blaming them on your partner or other people. Ask yourself, "What can I take more responsibility for here?"

I'm not saying you should blame yourself for things you *haven't* done, ignore your own hurt when people mistreat you, or deny injustice. Becoming a masochist isn't the answer—it's another facet of self-pity. If you find yourself on the receiving end of insults or aggression, this must be addressed when it's safe for you to do so. Enabling partners to behave in devaluing ways isn't good for you or them. You can recognize your needs and assert yourself while also facing your contribution to problems. Be humble without needless self-sacrifice. Tell the whole truth.

When you recognize your rumination cycles, you empower yourself. You're no longer at the mercy of anxious overthinking that's hidden and hard to spot. Identifying cycles deflates them, like bubbles you pop with a prick of needle-sharp awareness.

The next exercise will help you pick up on core themes in your ruminative thoughts as you identify your dominant and secondary rumination cycles.

SOLO EXERCISE: Rumination Cycles Log

At the top of a separate sheet of paper, or in a journal, make three columns with the headings "Triggers," "Associated Thoughts," and "Cycles." Then, think of a time when your threat link was activated (choose a situation where the activation was mild, a 1 or 2 on an intensity scale of 1 to 5). Write a brief five- to eight-word description of what happened under "Trigger." For example, if you recognize you get upset whenever your partner rearranges dishes you've loaded in the dishwasher, you might write "Joe rearranged the dishes I loaded" under "Trigger."

As you imagine yourself in this triggering situation, what kinds of repetitive negative thoughts did (or might) typically spin around in your mental pinwheel? Write down three or four examples. In the case of the rearranged dishes, you might write, "He corrects everything I do. He's controlling. He doesn't appreciate me," under "Associated Thoughts."

Sense into the theme of these thoughts. Do they carry an emotional charge of blame, control, doubt, worry, or self-pity? Write the cycle or cycles you've identified in the third column, under "Cycle(s)." There may be more than one cycle for each example.

Over the course of the next few days, fill out this log whenever you experience an upsetting event or situation with your partner. Once you've identified between six to ten triggers and cycles, put a star next to the cycle that shows up most on your list. This is likely your dominant rumination cycle. Underline the second most frequently recurring cycle. This is likely your secondary rumination cycle.

To download a PDF worksheet of this exercise, go to http://www.newharbinger.com/50034.

Relationship rumination, as you learned in this chapter, is a habit of chronic, repetitive, negative thinking engaged in by one or both partners within a committed, romantic bond. After reading this chapter, hopefully you have a better sense of how rumination in your relationship impacts both of your satisfaction levels, how to spot it, your primary and secondary rumination cycles, and their antidotes. The next step is to examine your relationship field.

CHAPTER 2

Your Relationship Field

You and your partner are connected in a psychic, emotional, spiritual, and energetic space. Physical limits don't define it. In the work of philosopher Martin Buber (2010), this space is called "the between." It's the foundation of all relations and relationships. Buddhist scholar Thich Nhat Hanh (2002) has called it "inter-being," emphasizing that "nothing has a separate self, and nothing exists by itself" (11). Because partners don't always *feel* connected, they can overlook the significance—and existence—of a relationship field.

Acknowledging that a relationship field exists requires a mental shift in how you view yourselves as a couple. It means recognizing that there's always more to both of you than meets the eye. Your unseen choices, decisions, actions, and impulses don't begin and end inside your skin. Even small, seemingly private choices have an impact.

When you throw garbage from the window of your car, it lands someplace—whether or not you see where. When you eat food, you're also eating the practices that went into creating, growing, harvesting, and transporting this food. When you drive your car without a muffler, toxic fumes linger in the air for others to breathe. You can pollute your relationship field with repetitive, negative thoughts, even when you're not aware of it.

The relationship field is a continuous, shifting, energetic ebb and flow of connection. It's here, between you and your partner: alive, vibrating, and responsive. It sends and receives information. You might even say that it *is* information. It adapts to new and different currents of energy, changing as you change, vibrating at frequencies you and your partner create together.

When you acknowledge the existence of this relationship field, you take an ecological view of thinking. Thoughts impact your partner's well-being and yours too. They can pollute or nourish your relational ecosystem. Shifting out of an individualistic paradigm into a relational one can transform the way you think about what you think. You'll see yourself as a contributor to the state of your relationship rather than as an innocent victim or a passive bystander. What you say or don't say—do or don't do—matters.

Responsibility has an upside. It fosters personal power and agency, giving you the confidence to support interdependence, healthy boundaries, and safety through your thinking, speech, and behaviors. If you regularly experience a sense of devitalization, boundary failures, and anxiety with your partner, rumination may be polluting your field.

Devitalization

In a relationship where one or both partners shut down, the energy of shifting and changing sensations, emotions and impulses can't flow easily or naturally. Partners ignore the messages and emotional signals their bodies send them. When energy doesn't flow, it can't be channeled creatively or productively. Imagine water trying to move through a garden hose full of kinks: eventually, the force of the water will pop the hose, spurt out in unexpected ways, and make a mess. Energy that can't flow builds up or stagnates. Sometimes, it seems to disappear until it explodes with destructive consequences.

Signs of devitalization in a relationship field are:

- feeling bored with each other

- joylessness

- an ongoing lack of creativity

- feeling uninspired

- existential angst

- low-grade depression

- an ongoing experience of deadness or numbness

- feeling trapped

- feeling cynical, jaded, or unmotivated

- purposelessness

- lack of passion

- feeling like roommates

- disconnection from yourself

- exhaustion.

Boundary Failures

When setting boundaries, it helps to have a strong sense of yourself as an individual, separate from your partner. It also helps when you can connect with your own genuine wants, needs, and desires. In order to set boundaries, you may have to make choices that go against what you've been told by your family, community, or society you *should* want, need, or desire. It takes courage to assert your boundaries when your own unconscious attachment system (more on this later in this chapter) drives you to stay connected and avoid making waves in a relationship.

Boundary-setting skills allow you to honor your own physical and mental health, even when it means disappointing others—including your partner—in the short term.

Signs of boundary failures in a relationship field include:

- making yourself responsible for your partner's choices, feelings, and actions

- chronic neediness and insecurity

- the expectation of mind-reading as a form of communication

- power imbalances

- mindlessly caretaking others

- passive aggression

- overreliance on rigid boundaries, structure, and routines

- feeling unmoored by too few boundaries, structure, or routines

- lack of commitment

- confusion about needs and wants

- inability to make decisions

- resentment

- feeling emotionally suffocated

- feeling controlled

- feeling like you can't live up to expectations

- believing your partner has to meet your expectations

- feeling emotionally disengaged from your partner.

If you regularly take too much responsibility for others as a way of coping with your own anxiety or discomfort, pay close attention to your motives. Why do you do this? Is it disorienting or frightening when you can't control the outcome of a situation? Do you feel obligated to keep the peace? What would happen if you only took responsibility for your own thoughts, feelings, choices, and behaviors in situations where you tend to overextend yourself?

If you take *too much* responsibility for what unfolds in your relationship field, you rob your partner of the opportunity to grow beyond their comfort zone, develop their relational skills, and see their contribution to relationship problems. When you practice setting and maintaining healthier boundaries, you recognize your *true* contribution to those things in your relationship that are hurting you. You don't turn your back on your own needs or overburden yourself with others' needs. You empower yourself and conserve energy you typically squander by releasing control of what isn't yours to control.

Anxiety

Imagine you can't rely on your partner to support you at key moments. Maybe you've learned it's not safe to lean on people and receive others' love and care. Or maybe your partner truly isn't capable of supporting you. Whatever the reasons, if you can't reduce your own stress—whether real or imagined—it becomes hard to relax. You could be blindsided or overwhelmed at any moment. As a result, you start doubting your own and your partner's ability to manage challenges. Doubt and distrust breed anxiety. If you can't relax, you can't release tension and reset your nervous system. Similar to driving a car with one foot on the brake pedal and one foot on the gas pedal, you will wear yourself out sooner than if you used one pedal at a time, either to brake because it's important to slow down or to accelerate because it's critical to move forward. Anxiety sets you at odds with yourself.

Signs of a relationship field saturated with anxiety are:

- irritability

- feeling obligated to stay together

- waiting for the other shoe to drop

- feeling unsafe, even when things are good

- excessive use of electronic devices

- excessive use of alcohol or other mind-altering substances

- inability to trust your partner

- expecting the worst

- having a hard time sleeping

- regular injuries, aches, and pains

- constant worrying

- difficulty opening up

- challenges being vulnerable

- lack of connection

- lack of intimacy.

Maintaining Your Field

If you and your partner see yourselves as co-contributors to the state of your relationship field, you increase your motivation to stop polluting it with ruminative thinking. You're clear that blaming stokes conflicts, controlling limits you, worrying can't fix the present, doubting destabilizes you, and self-pity promotes powerlessness. You're willing to acknowledge that what you say or don't say within a relationship field matters. So does what you do and don't do. The kind of thinking you indulge in influences your words and actions.

No matter who you are, you can make authentic, respectful connection a priority. Shifting from overthinking your experiences and defending against your vulnerabilities to *being with* them supports interdependence, healthier boundaries, and safety in your relationship field.

Interdependence

Being interdependent is the sweet spot between counterdependence—avoiding intimacy—and codependence—overrelying on another person for your sense of purpose, identity, and well-being. In a relationship field where two people cultivate interdependence, they both know and experience themselves as separate people while also feeling close and connected.

When you know and honor who you are separate from your partner, you're willing and able to make hard choices, take responsibility for yourself, and move in the direction of your deepest desires—whether for a date night or adopting a terrier together at the local shelter. In a relationship field where you and your partner respect each other's interdependence, you acknowledge that you are both agents of your own lives.

Being together is a choice. You accept your differences by supporting each other's right to be separate, distinct selves. At the same time, you are comfortable leaning on each other, relying on each other and needing each other.

Because you know where you end and your partner begins, you can also connect deeply and genuinely. Your partner's moods, feelings, needs, and desires may impact you, but they don't define you. Interdependence allows you to enjoy experiences of:

- being who you are

- appreciating your partner's quirks and imperfections

- feeling accepted even when you're not perfect

- feeling like anything is possible

- feeling happier with your partner in your life than without them in it

- feeling interested in each other

- feeling excitement when you're together

- feeling curious and fascinated by life

- feeling free (even though you're in a relationship)

- being comfortable leaning on and needing each other

- honestly advocating for yourself and your values

- challenging the status quo

- personal power

- creativity

- laughter and playfulness.

Healthy Boundaries

In her book *Set Boundaries, Find Peace: A Guide to Reclaiming Yourself,* Nedra Glover Tawwab (2021) describes three levels of boundaries: porous, rigid, and healthy. Porous boundaries are confusing, weak, or nonexistent. Rigid boundaries are immovable and unaccommodating. Healthy boundaries are clear, firm, and flexible. Partners with weak boundaries give others' needs priority over their own and are poor gatekeepers of their personal resources. Partners with rigid boundaries tend to be stubborn and guarded, which makes intimacy difficult. Partners with healthy boundaries can be firm while also being flexible.

Healthy boundaries are clear, reliable limits. They help you recognize and understand what works and what doesn't between you. They can help reduce anxiety because you know what's expected of you and how to meet those expectations. When old boundaries stop making sense and new ones are needed, limits can be reworked and renegotiated. Like highways, all boundaries require maintenance. Patching them, filling potholes, and sometimes overhauling them completely takes time and work. With so much traffic moving along them every day, boundaries are a critical part of the infrastructure of your relationship field.

When you cultivate healthy boundaries, you recognize that your partner is a unique being. They're not you. They're a different person. This seems obvious, but it's easy to forget. You make it a point to check in with them about what's okay with them and what's not okay.

Assumptions undermine healthy boundaries. If you're comfortable talking about your sexual identity, gender identity, fertility issues, or family history with friends and relatives, you know this doesn't automatically mean your partner is comfortable talking about these things as openly as you are. You ask them before sharing their personal information. You recognize and assert your boundaries while also researching and respecting theirs.

In a relationship field with healthy boundaries, you enjoy:

- being heard and respected
- saying "no" when you mean "no"

- saying "yes" when you mean "yes"

- clarity about what your partner needs, wants, and expects—and why

- not having to guess when it comes to pleasing your partner

- being able to make mistakes and learn

- being able to pivot and change direction

- experiencing appropriate guilt or shame when you cross or disregard boundaries

- helping each other get through feelings of guilt and shame

- being held accountable firmly when boundaries are crossed or disregarded

- being able to count on clear and consistent limits

- open discussions about boundaries

- boundary renegotiation when needs and desires change.

When you want to establish healthy boundaries with your partner, keep these guideposts in mind.

1. Bring to mind a boundary you want to establish. For example, "I'd like you to wait till I'm done speaking before offering me your thoughts or opinions about what I'm saying."

2. Connect with the "why" behind this boundary. How will this boundary support you and your relationship?

3. Use positive rather than negative language to acknowledge the intention behind your boundary. For example, "I want to feel safe and comfortable sharing my thoughts with you," rather than, "I want to be with someone who isn't selfish and doesn't interrupt me."

4. Honor your boundary through action, such as restating your boundary or giving your partner what Tawwab (2021) calls "a

healthy ultimatum." An example of a healthy ultimatum might be, "The next time you interrupt me, I'll refrain from sharing whatever it was I wanted to share at that moment." Accept that your partner's choices and decisions regarding your boundaries are beyond your control. If you can't accommodate and also honor one another's boundaries and still be true to yourselves, you may need to reevaluate your goals and priorities as a couple.

Safety

Safety allows you to trust yourself, your partner, and your relationship. When you make mistakes, your partner disappoints you, or unexpected events blindside you, trust can be restored. If there's a baseline of safety in your relationship, it strengthens your sense of who you are, who your partner is, and who you are together. At the same time, a strong sense of yourselves as individuals and as a couple fosters a sense of safety. Paradoxically, partners who feel safe can take calculated risks, investing themselves in adventures and opportunities.

In a relationship field where emotional and physical safety are the norm, you appreciate:

- taking informed and calculated risks

- regularly stepping out of your comfort zones

- knowing you have each other's back

- time spent with your partner

- periods of time away from your partner

- a steady stream of new learnings and insights

- experiencing and resolving conflicts rather than avoiding them

- knowing that tough moments are temporary

- genuine repair as a common occurrence

- your partner making your well-being a top priority.

By recognizing your contribution to the state of something bigger than both of you—the relationship field you cocreate—you can foster emotional resilience and forge an alliance in service of a shared goal: maintaining a relationship field where interdependence, healthy boundaries, and safety can evolve and flourish.

As you acknowledge and care for your relationship and reduce rumination, there's one key factor you don't want to overlook: your attachment style.

Attachment Styles in the Field

The four-category model of adult attachment incorporates earlier models and proposes four primary attachment styles: secure, anxious, avoidant-dismissive, and avoidant-fearful (Bartholomew and Horowitz 1991). Here, I focus mostly on three styles: secure, anxious, and avoidant (this last style combines elements of both the avoidant-dismissive and avoidant-fearful styles described by Bartholomew and Horowitz). Once we've considered individual attachment styles and how these shape ruminative thinking in relationships, we'll look at how your attachment style combines with your partner's into what I call an "attachment style pairing" or ASP. ASPs represent the interplay of attachment styles partners create together, and they can influence relationship rumination. For this reason, it helps to understand your ASP.

British psychologist John Bowlby (1986) first began formulating attachment theory eighty years ago. Since then, research has shown how early bonds with primary caregivers shape how children act later as adults in relationships. Fears and longings originating in your earliest formative attachments fire up memories, physiological responses, and emotions. They also activate unconscious interpersonal templates about love. Implicit in these templates are expectations of danger and reward. These unconscious expectations seeded in the past come alive full force in present-day romantic commitments, setting into motion outdated coping strategies you used as a child to ensure your physical and psychic survival.

In *Attached,* authors Levine and Heller (2010) note, "The need to be near someone special is so important that the brain has a biological mechanism specifically responsible for creating and regulating our connection with our attachment figures" (12). This mechanism is our attachment system. When you're triggered by something your partner says or does, this system fires up, and things can get emotionally charged and intense. The reason this happens is partly because your brain isn't too different now than it was between thirty-five thousand and a hundred thousand years ago. You respond to triggers in your relationship as intensely as if you were facing a tiger or deadly assassin (Neubauer et al. 2018). A threat to your romantic alliance—even a small one—can feel like a threat to your survival.

So what does it mean to have a secure, anxious, or avoidant attachment style?

Secure Attachment

Secure attachment is often distorted into the stereotype we associate with romantic love. A couple clinks champagne glasses on a balcony and snaps selfies in front of the Taj Mahal. Young lovers lie in bed half naked as they gaze into each other's eyes. Idealized and taken out of context, the myth of "natural," effortless secure attachment contributes to relationship rumination. It showcases a simplistic version of partnership, where it's easy to believe that all you have to do to be happy as a couple is win a magical, lucky love lottery.

But this stereotype isn't realistic or attainable. When partners aspire to it, they mistake normal relationship difficulties and challenges as signs of personal failure. As the happy-hour love cocktail of oxytocin, dopamine, and serotonin drains away, lovers free fall through cloud nine and land with a jolt on the asphalt of their ordinary, everyday lives. Rent or mortgage payments are due. Laundry accumulates. Diapers don't change themselves. In-laws criticize furniture choices. Careless partners leave facial hair in the sink. Differences emerge.

This is normal.

Securely attached people don't have perfect relationships. They struggle. They fantasize about leaving. They shut down and cling. But because they're generally more relaxed about closeness and have more experience setting healthy boundaries, they tend to deal directly with challenges as they arise and have a more varied and flexible repertoire of coping styles and strategies than their avoidant or anxious counterparts. They cling less and avoid less. They're better at handling the uncertainties of emotional attachments without over- or underreacting.

Secure may be your attachment style if:

- you generally trust the experience of partnership

- you enjoy connecting with your partner, though you can also be by yourself

- you're pretty good at tolerating the uncertainty and vulnerability that go with relying on another grown adult for attention and care

- you can relax into the ups and downs of loving

- you can accept the experience of having a range of positive and negative feelings toward your partner, sometimes at the same time

- when your partner isn't available, you can soothe yourself

- when you fight, you can make up, even if you don't always do it perfectly.

Flowing in and out of connection is a constant in all couples' lives. Over time, couples who put in the work can get better at this flow, and conflicts become milder and less frequent. Repairs can happen more quickly and efficiently. A peaceful alliance can become your baseline.

If you have an anxious attachment style, you'll most likely need to invest time and effort into developing some of the skills that come more naturally to those with a secure style.

Anxious Attachment

Anxiously attached people seek proximity. Their fears increase when they're with a partner who wants more physical or emotional distance than they do. They try to achieve or maintain close contact with their partner by worrying, strategizing, and controlling situations in ways that keep their partner within their orbit. If this is your style, your triggers will center around your partner's unavailability and distance-seeking behaviors.

Anxious may be your attachment style if:

- you choose partners you believe you can control

- it hurts that your partner doesn't include you more in things they do

- you resent their pursuits and hobbies

- you have a hard time accepting your partner's friendships

- your partner's job raises your anxiety level

- whatever separates you from your partner feels like a potential threat

- your partner frequently makes plans without informing you till the last minute

- you don't ever get enough attention, affection, or understanding from your partner.

Your partner's emotional unavailability is a major relationship trigger that sets off rumination cycles focused on your need for closeness. If you blame yourself for your partner's standoffishness, your overthinking may take the form of a blame cycle that revolves around your own neediness, your partner's distancing behaviors, or your sadness. If you blame your partner, your cycles will focus on your partner's flaws, their inadequacies, and the ways they cause you pain and disappoint you. You may also judge them for failing to love you the "right" way.

Worry cycles spin around future worst-case scenarios: potential losses, unfulfilled dreams, imagined regrets. Control cycles feature recurring thoughts about managing your partner's attention or getting them to appreciate you or fully commit to you or the relationship. Doubt cycles undermine your certainty about what you know or intuit. Self-pity cycles reinforce the belief that your partner is selfish or immature while you are an innocent victim of the relationship awaiting rescue.

Lisette (in chapter 1) leans toward an anxious attachment style. After they eat dinner, she typically says, "I'm tired," and leaves Manuel alone in the living room when what she truly wants is more affection from him. He turns on the television to watch football. Lisette sits on her bed spinning a self-pity cycle, hoping Manuel will worry about her, come to the door, and ask if she's okay. When he doesn't, she feels unsettled and panicky. In the end, she usually ends up opening the door to their bedroom and saying, "Can you please turn down the TV?"

Avoidant Attachment

Unlike anxious partners, who were left to their own devices when they needed support, avoidantly attached partners usually have a history of being intruded upon or controlled when they needed space. If you're on the avoidant side of the attachment spectrum, you have a hard time trusting that being close to another person won't result in your boundaries being trampled.

Avoidant may be your attachment style if:

- in your early life, something interfered with your healthy drive to establish yourself as separate and distinct from a caregiver

- you were discouraged from expressing and pursuing your own needs

- you use emotional distancing techniques to reduce your anxiety in relationships

- you idealize solitude and "alone time"

- intimacy can feel threatening and anxiety provoking

- you'd rather hedge commitment than risk letting your partner down

- "alone time" is often code for "time away from my partner with other people who don't make emotional demands on me."

Your triggers center around times when your partner wants to know more than you're willing to disclose about work, feelings, thoughts, friends, family, plans for the future, past experiences, hobbies, dreams, interests, food, travel, or musical and artistic preferences. You wish your partner would accept the information you volunteer without asking follow-up questions. You don't like it when your partner tries to connect with you when what you need is space and silence. They want more verbal and physical expressions of affection from you than you're able to comfortably give them. You experience your partner as needy.

Remember Eddie, who feels uncomfortable when Chandra tells him she loves him? Because his attachment style is avoidant, Chandra's affection becomes an overarching relationship trigger for him. So does her need for his attention. Eddie can easily slip into blame cycles when Chandra asks him to hold her hand when they're out in public. *She's so controlling. She's suffocating me. I wish she'd leave me alone.* Eddie can also blame himself. *I'm no good at relationships. I can't give her what she wants. Maybe I just don't know how to love.* In his doubt cycles, he wonders, *Will I ever be happy? Is fulfillment possible? What if I'm not cut out for any of this?* In self-pity cycles, he feels like Chandra's victim: *She's too demanding. It's not fair. Why do I always end up with needy women?*

When Eddie indulges in control cycles, he rehashes thoughts about what to share with Chandra and what to withhold in order to manage her reactions to him. *If I tell her about my trip, she'll get mad. Better keep it private. I won't go into any details about my plans with my family over the holidays, otherwise she'll expect me to invite her.* The more Eddie seeks safety and invulnerability by withholding his plans, feelings, needs, desires, and fears from Chandra, the more he fills their relationship field with toxic omissions.

SOLO EXERCISE: Attachment Style Assessment

To explore your own attachment style, reflect on the following pairs of state-ments. For each pair, select only *one* statement: don't choose a statement that reflects how you *wish* you felt—choose the most accurate one. If both statements in each pair seem to apply to you equally, sense into which one reflects your deepest emotional needs.

Write the letter that represents your selection in your journal or down-load the PDF worksheet for this exercise from http://www.newharbinger .com/50034.

A.   I have a need to be closer to my partner than I am.

B.   I have a need for more space and time to myself in my relationship.

A.   I wish I knew more about my partner's thoughts, feelings, or inner world.

B.   Respecting privacy and separateness is a priority for me in relationships.

A.   I wish we did more fun things together as a couple.

B.   Having freedom to pursue your own interests helps sustain a relationship.

A.   It feels like I can handle anything as long as my partner and I stay connected.

B.   Connection takes a lot of effort and energy, and I'm not always sure I'm doing it right.

A.   I feel most relaxed when my partner reassures me of their commitment.

B.   I feel most relaxed when there's no pressure to make hard and fast commitments.

More A answers than B answers suggests you lean toward an anxious attachment style. More B answers than A answers suggests you lean toward an avoidant attachment style.

Attachment Style Pairings

Couples can benefit from understanding their attachment style pairing (ASP). Your ASP is the dynamic combination of your two individual attachment styles. It can influence the interplay of your relationship triggers and factor into the frequency and intensity of your rumination cycles.

Understandably, conflicts with partners often feel deeply personal. Despite originating in the past, attachment styles still influence you as a couple by feeding into common conflicts that virtually all couples with your ASP also struggle with. By viewing conflicts through the lens of your ASP, you take a step back from disagreements, allow the dust to settle, and focus on how long-standing attachment styles have shaped you as people.

When you pursue, cling, or withdraw, your amygdala is still attaching code-red signals to bygone dangers and threats. Sometimes these dangers are present with your partner. Now, as an adult, you have resources that were unavailable to you as a child. You couldn't choose your early caregivers, but you can (and do) choose your partner. Can you *be with* the discomfort evoked by their desire for closeness or distance rather than overthinking it?

Anxious-Avoidant

The anxious-avoidant attachment style pairing sets partners up for an unfortunate self-fulfilling prophecy, unless they take steps toward a more secure-secure pairing. The anxious partner's rumination cycles are set into motion by their avoidant partner's emotional distancing.

Repetitive negative thinking in the anxiously attached partner's mind leaks into the relationship field as aggressive energy, critical words, and controlling behaviors. If the avoidant partner also ruminates, their repetitive negative thinking will leak into the relationship field too.

Most fights in the anxious-avoidant ASP follow a predictable pattern. The anxious partner wants more closeness, and the avoidant partner shuts down and becomes less responsive. The anxious partner doubles down on blaming, criticism, or self-pity, hoping to reengage their partner. For the anxious partner, even a negative reaction is better than their avoidant partner's apparent indifference. In a vicious cycle, the avoidant partner withdraws further and barricades themselves internally as their beliefs are confirmed about their boundaries being recklessly disregarded. As a last resort, they may yell, insult their partner, or threaten to leave, hoping to create the space they need to feel safe again by scaring their partner away. The anxious partner's beliefs are thereby confirmed that their partner is mean, selfish, or unreliable.

Eddie and Chandra fit the profile for the anxious-avoidant ASP. The difference between the icing-covered love cake Chandra dreamed of when her roommate introduced them and the crumbs she gets leaves her love-starved and spinning blame cycles directed mostly at herself: *Why am I so insecure? Why can't I be happy? I'm driving him away. What's wrong with me?*

Eddie senses Chandra's dissatisfaction. Her low-grade, free-floating unhappiness fills the air when they're together like spores of mold. He finds it hard to breathe around her. He tries to spend his free time with friends, whenever he can come up with an excuse to do something without her. Over time, Chandra's rumination cycles shift from self-blame to worry and control cycles. She starts going through Eddie's text messages and following his friends on social media platforms, looking for evidence that he's cheating on her.

As you practice SLOW in upcoming chapters, you'll learn to see when your interactions resemble Chandra and Eddie's and how to shift this ASP dynamic. You'll also begin seeing and labeling your thoughts and rumination cycles so you can interrupt them. When you open to vulnerabilities fueling ruminative thoughts, you can *be with* emotional pain more often rather than sidestepping it in ways that fuel your suffering. You can also welcome your own vulnerabilities as a valuable part of who you are. This makes it easier to respond to triggers calmly and move toward a more secure-secure ASP.

Avoidant-Avoidant

People with an entrenched avoidant attachment style don't generally pair up for long. Two people with an avoidant-dismissive attachment style might go on a few dates, enjoy each other's company for a while, or have a passionate sexual connection, but as soon as things start getting serious, they usually lose interest. They minimize or devalue the importance of commitment, ghost each other, cancel dates, or insist the relationship is too heavy or constricting and they need time apart to figure things out.

When people end up in an avoidant-avoidant ASP, one person usually leans toward avoidant-dismissive while their partner leans toward avoidant-fearful. In avoidant-dismissive attachment, the importance of partnership is minimized, dismissed, or denied. In avoidant-fearful attachment, loving feels vulnerable—and terrifying—since rejection, pain, and loss are associated with vulnerability.

Bernadette and Rajid begin their relationship in this attachment style pairing. Bernadette is avoidant-dismissive, and Rajid is avoidant-fearful. They live in different cities. They've been seeing each other once a month for a year. Rajid wishes he could visit Bernadette more often, though he doesn't bring this up with her. The inner conflict he experiences between his desire for more contact and his fear of vulnerability sets off regular rumination cycles of doubt and worry.

Most guys would envy me. We have great sex when I see her, and the rest of the time, I'm free as a bird. Or am I lying to myself? Is she toying with me? I know she sees other guys too. At least she's honest. There are no strings attached, so why can't I forget about her?

When Rajid admits he wants to spend more time with Bernadette, she says, "That's sweet, and I'm flattered, but I told you I don't want anything serious."

Avoidant-dismissive partners don't usually engage in the same degree of relationship rumination as partners who fit the avoidant-fearful or anxious attachment styles. Their style tends to keep them on the fringes of committed romantic relationships. If they do end up committing to someone, they will often still privately consider themselves single. This was the case with Margo, whom you may remember from chapter 1. She spun control cycles justifying her choice to withhold information from Kerri when she met up with an attractive colleague after work. What many avoidant-dismissive partners believe—and don't say out loud—is "I'll keep up appearances and fulfill my role, but the real me will remain hidden."

Both avoidant-dismissive and avoidant-fearful partners can develop a more secure attachment style over time. By recognizing their ASP, they can bring attention to their own relationship-minimizing or intimacy-avoidant behaviors. They can notice and question their ruminative thought cycles rather than blindly accepting them as true. Partners who share this style can explore the deeper fears and needs underlying their distance-seeking thoughts and behaviors rather than buying into the comfortable narrative that "I'm just the way I am."

Anxious-Anxious

Both people in an anxious-anxious attachment style pairing cling to each other to create safety. They have a hard time functioning independently. Everyday tasks and responsibilities like shopping or going to work can be challenging for partners in this ASP.

When Vince and Ronald first met, they thought they'd found a safe haven in their relationship. They'd both been with avoidant partners before. Loneliness and frustration were the norm for them in relationships. Their mutual attachment was a new experience and a huge relief. But the fears fueling their rumination cycles hadn't gone away. Despite their mutual need for each other, they continued to cling and control, just as they had with their avoidant exes.

Ronald's diet became a trigger for Vince. When Ronald binged on processed foods, it set off Vince's rumination cycles of control, blame, and self-pity: *He eats so poorly. He has high blood pressure. If he really loved me, he'd be healthier. I need to go through everything in our pantry and throw out all the junk. Why won't he do everything he can to change for us?* Arguments centered around Vince being paranoid and controlling and Ronald being irresponsible and self-destructive.

Ronald also feared something terrible would happen to Vince, which spiked his anxiety. Whenever Vince left for work, images of all the catastrophes that might prevent him from returning home flooded Ronald's mind. He pictured viruses infecting him, car accidents, and renegade gunmen, and then comforted himself by eating fast food and sugary snacks.

Vince and Ronald's rumination cycles kept spinning until they started learning how to be with their fear of loss and abandonment rather than defending against it with overthinking.

Anxious-Secure

In an anxious-secure attachment style pairing, it takes time for the anxiously attached partner to develop trust. Repeated positive experiences with a more securely attached partner can tip the scale. If you're the securely attached person in this ASP, remaining patient and understanding will be your challenge. It can be hard to do this while also setting limits and honoring your own needs.

The rumination cycles of anxiously attached partners often have little to do with their securely attached partner's experience of themselves. Anxiously attached people will react to their own repetitive, negative thinking when they're out of touch with their partner's actual intentions.

An anxiously attached person involved with a securely attached partner can reduce their overthinking by recognizing their triggers. They can also see their rumination cycles. Anxiously attached people can reduce their anxiety by learning how to *be with* what's happening in the moment and making peace with their own vulnerabilities and attachment needs instead of chronically thinking their way out of

discomfort. You'll learn how to do this more often when you're introduced to SLOW in chapters 4 through 7.

Trudy and Sean fit this ASP profile. Initially, Trudy found Sean
"boring." She hadn't dated a man with a secure attachment style before.
He was even-keeled and confident.

Her rumination cycles tended toward doubt and worry: *What if I
don't love him? What if he doesn't love me? I'm not sure we feel any real
attraction. My ex was horrible, but the sex was great. What if I'm settling
with Sean? Sure, this is easy and comfortable—but is this love?*

After six months of dating, Trudy broke up with Sean. She told him
she wanted more passion. After dating several other men with avoidant
attachment styles, though, she realized she'd mistaken adrenaline-fueled
drama for passion. When she reached out for Sean, expressed regret for
breaking up with him, and told him she wanted to try again, he'd already
moved on.

Because Sean's expectations in a relationship were more balanced
than what Trudy was used to, he hadn't set off the same painful rumination cycles she'd come to associate with love in prior romantic attachments. Secure attachment with Sean had felt weirdly normal. Despite
losing Sean, Trudy found herself increasingly attracted to partners with
secure attachment styles. She had started to appreciate the safety and
trust she'd experienced in an anxious-secure ASP.

Avoidant-Secure

In an avoidant-secure attachment style pairing, the securely attached
person doesn't overreact to the avoidantly attached partner's distancing
behaviors in the same way anxiously attached partners do. If the avoidantly attached person finds this new dynamic uncomfortable, they may
act out. This can provoke the secure partner to react in anxious, critical,
or angry ways that echo the reactions of an anxiously attached partner
in the same situation.

The avoidantly attached person in this ASP may find themselves
experiencing more freedom and trust with a partner who gives them
plenty of space while remaining steady and reliable. If they're used to

anxiously attached partners threatening to leave and then clinging to them, a securely attached partner's moderate, measured, or rational responses at key moments can lead the avoidantly attached partner to begin revising their fear-based view of love.

Over time, as experiences rooted in secure attachment happen more often, contradicting the avoidantly attached partner's fear-based rumination, their style can soften. They may begin to learn and use a wider range of responses in formerly triggering moments and situations.

This was the case with Wilson and Ella. Since his early teens, Wilson had dated women who wanted more time, attention, closeness, and intimacy than he could give. These relationships had been undermined by rumination cycles, judgment, criticism, and passive-aggressive comments and behaviors. Negatively charged relationship fields crackling with contempt and hostility were all Wilson knew. When he started dating Ella, he dreaded the moment when he would reveal he'd planned a mountain climbing trip with some friends.

Shockingly, Ella's response was, "Have a good time!" He thought it was a trick. When he returned, she was curious about his adventure. Wilson braced himself for Ella's resentful actions, snide comments, and love-withdrawal. Instead, she remained affectionate. Gradually, Wilson stopped expecting negative reactions whenever he went away and did his own thing.

Ella generally felt pretty safe in relationships. She believed Wilson enjoyed her company but knew he also enjoyed his time alone or with friends. Although she didn't need time away as much as he did, she did enjoy it too on occasion. This didn't mean she was compliant or didn't speak up when Wilson hurt her. When he was inconsiderate or irresponsible, she expressed her feelings directly and asked him to adjust his behavior. She also made it a point to regularly let him know she genuinely appreciated him.

At first, Wilson feared Ella didn't really love him. He thought love and possessiveness were the same thing. Being loved rather than controlled felt unfamiliar. It took time to trust that Ella wasn't going to shame him for regularly seeking out his own space. Although he continued to plan trips alone and with friends, his bandwidth for intimacy with Ella increased. He relaxed into the safety of their relationship field and started to enjoy low-drama loving.

Secure-Secure

In a secure-secure attachment style pairing:

- partners can be both independent and dependent

- partners see themselves as allies who are on the same team

- they don't hide or disguise their vulnerabilities

- they acknowledge and voice fears, needs, and wants

- they work to understand their partner's perspective

- they willingly adapt and grow

- the relationship field of partners in this ASP supports interdependence, healthy boundaries, and safety

- expressive, toxic omission, and energetic leakages lessen over time.

Partners with this ASP are less prone to overthinking their relationship because the way they feel, express themselves, and act is in sync with their attachment needs. Most of the time, they don't let their fears of being judged or rejected overpower their commitment to voicing what's true for them. They also don't use honesty as an excuse for being unkind or disrespectful. They can communicate directly with one another and share needs, fears, and vulnerabilities rather than getting sidetracked by rumination cycles.

When something sets them off, secure partners don't brood too long about what their partner did wrong or what they could have done better. They see their partner's errors and flaws, but they also look at their contribution to problems.

Choose Your ASP Adventure

In all the attachment style pairs, there are three possible outcomes:

1. Partners move toward (or sustain) a secure-secure attachment dynamic.

2. Partners move in the direction of a more turbulent or detached dynamic.

3. One or both partners leave, and the relationship ends.

In a secure-secure ASP, both partners trust love. Maybe not 100 percent, maybe not always, but mostly and often. They can relax into the uncertainties inherent in relationships. Rather than clinging to a moment of happiness or to an idealized partner, they work with and accept the ebb and flow of their own and their partner's changing moods and circumstances. Nothing stays the same. Conflicts and disappointments are a part of loving. They give up the fantasy of achieving a fixed state of unchanging, eternal bliss.

Instead of avoiding discomfort, partners in secure-secure ASPs get better at coping with discomfort, on their own and as a couple. They make conscious communication a habit, speaking and listening honestly and respectfully as the rule rather than the exception. They repair after conflicts, recognize their part in disconnections, learn from mistakes, and do what they need to do to move past grievances. Partners in a secure-secure ASP navigate togetherness and separation within a relationship field where interdependence, healthy boundaries, and safety are priorities.

Research shows attachment styles aren't absolute. Sometimes, they're even relationship-specific. Wilson and Ella grew into a more secure-secure ASP. Through her experiences with Sean, Trudy's anxious style shifted toward secure. One study conducted at the University of Ottawa examining participants' attachments across a range of relationships— parents, friends, and romantic partners—suggests that attachment patterns can be context-specific (Caron et al. 2012). Try visualizing attachment styles as a spectrum with "secure" in the middle and "anxious" and "avoidant" on either end. Your position on the spectrum may be a little different in different relationships. Should you recognize you're on one end while your partner is on the other end, each of you can take steps to move toward more secure middle ground.

Anxious	Secure	Avoidant
⇒	————————————	⇐

Although they're not set in stone, attachment styles are also not fleeting. They're your internal working models of relationships reinforced through countless interactions with others, often over decades. Unlike passing moods or preferences, they won't come and go easily. Don't expect them to change overnight. Old patterns transform when new, secure interpersonal experiences repeatedly contradict them and establish a new pattern.

As you shift across the attachment spectrum, be compassionate with yourself and your partner. Neither of you chose your attachment style. It's how you learned to cope with pain and fear. The attachment style you developed was the "best" (and sometimes only) option for sustaining connection with people you needed as a child. You related with the caregivers you depended on for your physical and emotional survival by clinging, pursuing, minimizing your own needs, meeting these needs indirectly, or blocking intrusive connection however you could.

Shifting your style along the attachment spectrum will take time. How much time will depend on the personal healing work you do and the support you get. Don't fall into rumination cycles about it when your ASP patterns resurface. Being aware of your ASP is a step toward shifting into more secure-secure territory. Whatever ASP describes your joint styles best, celebrate your willingness to acknowledge your pairing and take small steps to change your dynamic. Consider secure attachment a practice, not a destination.

Growth occurs over time. It's rarely linear. Whenever you're separated from your partner and you manage to soothe yourself, it's a win.

Whenever you negotiate anxiety-provoking periods of closeness or distance calmly and kindly, it's another win. Whenever you let go of clinging or avoiding, even if only for a few breaths, that's also a win.

Your relationship history doesn't have to dictate how you act now. What you see as a failure in the moment may be a win in the making if you can step back and take the long view.

JOINT EXERCISE: Our Working ASP

Review the attachment style assessment both of you completed earlier in this chapter. Write down your attachment styles, separated by a dash. This is your working ASP, a shorthand for the underlying needs and fears that clash, at times, and set off rumination cycles. Use your ASP as an awareness tool. Revise it when your dynamic changes.

Reflect on the following questions or share your answers with your partner (refer to the Speaker and Listener responsibilities in the introduction if you need a refresher on creating safety and supporting connection).

* What's one way that understanding your ASP could help when a threat link gets activated, especially by your desire for more closeness or more space?

* How can keeping your ASP in mind help you take conflicts less personally?

* What's one thing you can do to move toward a more secure-secure ASP?

In this chapter, you learned about the relationship field. If unchecked, rumination pollutes it, leading to devitalization, boundary failures, and anxiety. Reducing rumination, on the other hand, supports interdependence, healthy boundaries, and safety in your field. You've been introduced to three basic attachment styles—anxious, avoidant, and secure—and five attachment style pairings (ASPs): anxious-avoidant, avoidant-avoidant, anxious-secure, avoidant-secure, and secure-secure.

ASPs factor into the frequency and intensity of rumination. Although they don't change overnight, you can develop a more secure-secure ASP.

In the next chapter, you'll explore one of the most influential factors in successfully reducing overthinking: your mindset.

CHAPTER 3

The Foundational Mindset of SLOW

Our mindset influences our attitudes, beliefs, and values. Conversely, our attitudes, beliefs, and values influence our mindset. A difference in mindset between two couples can be what accounts for the same crisis impacting them in opposite ways. An affair, for example, can lead partners into recurring cycles of blame, attack, and counterattack with devastating consequences. But there are also partners whose mindset allows them to view an affair—over time—with a solemn kind of gratitude, despite the emotional pain thinking about it may continue evoking in them.

Couples can change their mindset in order to overcome sexual blocks and revitalize their relationship when passion has dwindled. A new mindset may help them renew their commitment to each other rather than living parallel lives when their children have grown up and left the house. A crisis can challenge partners to show up for themselves and each other vulnerably, see what's true for them, and reconnect with their priorities as a couple.

Your mindset is one of the most influential factors in reducing relationship rumination. It shapes how you handle and perceive setbacks. It determines whether or not you commit to new practices, tools, and techniques or whether you fall back on old, familiar ways of thinking and coping. Your mindset will shape the successes you experience and the way you perceive obstacles and disappointments as you learn and start using SLOW—the practice of interrupting rumination through seeing, labeling, opening, and welcoming.

A Fixed Mindset

Psychologist Carol Dweck (2007) proposes that people operate from one of two primary mindsets: fixed and growth. If you have a fixed mindset, you view people and situations as fixed and unchanging. You see the world a certain way. No matter what people do or don't do, you believe they stay the same. Fixed mindsets reinforce beliefs like "I'm just the way I am." Conversely, beliefs like "I'm just the way I am" reinforce fixed mindsets. Either way, with a fixed mindset, you believe "Things don't change" and "Life is the way I see it."

None of us assumes a fixed mindset out of ill will. Nobody wants to inhibit their own growth. At the same time, if you've developed a fixed mindset, it will reinforce black-and-white thinking and inflexible expectations of yourself, others, and your relationship. Even though you may not have intentionally set your mind this way, it's your responsibility to reset it to support new growth.

Why do I need to change? What's the point of questioning my beliefs? There's a good reason I see the world the way I do. Is this really the right approach?

It's not uncommon to experience doubt cycles when you open yourself to a growth mindset. When partners with fixed mindsets try to learn something new, they may feel confused and threatened. Someone who has mostly approached life with a fixed mindset isn't going to instantly let go of the power, strength, and control that seems to accompany being an expert, knowing what's "right" or having the answers. Opening up to a new approach that involves "not knowing" is a process. If you can *be with* the doubt cycles that surface while you shift your mindset rather than getting lost in the content of your thinking, you'll support yourself in opening up to a new, more flexible way of perceiving things.

Your default mindset may be "fixed" if:

- You view people and situations as fixed and unchanging.

- You have little faith in growth and self-improvement.

- You see things in binary terms: people either can or can't do things.

- You believe individual people (as well as entire categories of people) have unchanging traits or characteristics that shape how they behave and who they are at their core (for example, "rich people are bad," "men can't be nurturing," "neighbors are nosy").

- When considering making a change, you think, *It's too late,* or *It's too hard.*

- Many of your views fit in opposing categories: right or wrong, good or bad, healthy or unhealthy.

- When your partner asks you to change, you dismiss it with, *I am the way I am.*

- When your partner tries to change, you dismiss it with, *They are the way they are.*

- You view small positive changes as too little or irrelevant.

A Growth Mindset

A growth mindset helps you see possibilities in difficult situations. It sets you up to recognize and enjoy small wins—those moments when you do something new that supports positive change. Over time, small wins accumulate to make a big difference. Seeing learning opportunities in so-called problems, errors, failures, mistakes, and challenges is the essence of learning. Because undoing rumination isn't a goal you accomplish with a one-time flip of a switch, you'll do better when you can enjoy small wins along the way without getting hung up on inevitable setbacks and disappointments.

Shifting into a growth mindset makes it easier to practice SLOW, especially when you actively work on being patient, curious, and nonattached. This is because practicing SLOW involves being willing to let go of whatever it is you *think* you know about a situation or experience in favor of discovering what you're not fully aware of yet.

You may already approach life with a growth mindset if:

- You see learning opportunities in so-called mistakes, setbacks, and problems.

- You believe both you and your partner can change to improve your relationship.

- You aspire to interdependence, healthy boundaries, and safety with your partner.

- You believe all people are capable of growing at any point in their life.

- You see potential for positive change in difficult situations.

- You rarely see situations, people, and events in binary terms.

- You appreciate how complex people and situations can be.

- You value small positive changes as "wins" and celebrate them.

Shifting into a growth mindset makes it easier to practice SLOW because it primes you for learning and discovery. It prepares you to accept that people and situations are more complex than they may appear, and you trust that lasting change unfolds organically even as you invite and support it with ordinary, everyday choices. Because you're not expecting immediate success on your terms and timeline, you're less likely to give up on growth prematurely.

SOLO EXERCISE: My Small Wins

Small wins are moments when you do something that supports positive change even when it's uncomfortable for you. A small win is choosing to get grounded in one breath rather than reacting to a surly tone you've picked up on in your partner's voice. It's getting genuinely curious about your partner's frustration instead of losing yourself in defensiveness. It's noticing that when your partner doesn't replace the toilet paper roll, it's a trigger for you. It's identifying one of your rumination cycles. It's choosing to *be with* an internal experience rather than chronically *thinking about* what has triggered you.

In your journal, write "My Small Wins" at the top of a page. Underneath, write the word "Today" at the beginning of five or six lines in a column moving down the page. Then, record a few of your recent small wins after the word "Today." For example, you might write, "Today I noticed that when no one changes the toilet paper roll, it's a trigger for me" or "Today I recognized I slipped into a self-pity cycle when my wife went biking with friends."

Add to this list every day and read it regularly. For a PDF worksheet of this exercise, go to http://www.newharbinger.com/50034.

Checking Your Mindset

Most lasting psychological change follows the two-steps-forward-one-step-back model. With a fixed mindset, you may misinterpret the one-step-back moments as failures. But what if every step back is actually an essential prelude to your next step forward?

As you work through this book, check your mindset whenever you get stuck. If you feel frustrated, reread the list of characteristics of a fixed mindset. Do any items on the list describe how you're perceiving your progress? Reread the characteristics of a growth mindset. Are you willing to trust how your experience is unfolding so you can learn or discover something new?

You may need to embrace a growth mindset many times as you open up to *not* knowing and to changing in small increments—especially when you begin the SLOW process outlined in chapters 4 through 7. Being patient and curious will help you shift out of a fixed mindset. So will letting go of the belief that growth must happen as you envision it and on your timeline.

Patience

Sex educator Emily Nagoski (2015) calls the mental feedback loop between what we want and how soon we expect to get it "the monitor." Drawing on the research of Charles Carver and Michael Scheier (2012,

2013), Nagoski proposes that this internal "monitor" is satisfied when you reach your goals on your own timeline and frustrated when you don't. Your monitor assesses how close (or far) you are from your desires and whether or not you believe your efforts are being rewarded quickly enough. It reacts to how long it takes you to reach your goals in comparison with how long you think it *should* take. Although it's normal to want things when you want them, if you can't adjust your internal monitor when obstacles arise, you are more likely to give up on your goals prematurely, out of frustration.

Personal growth can be stressful for people with overzealous monitors. People who want to improve their relationship may interpret their seeming lack of progress as a failure. But changing the dynamics in your relationships—as well as changing your own mental patterns—isn't the same thing as changing your wardrobe or your job. Inflexible goals and timelines undermine progress. When it comes to being with your own vulnerabilities and fears, you can't coerce change. You can't pry yourself open like an oyster and force your unconscious to give you its pearls. If you want to reduce rumination and nurture love, patience is important. Most lasting change takes time.

Being patient with your own change process requires you to let go while also holding on. Learning to be patient as you practice SLOW will balance the urgency of wanting everything to improve for the better ASAP with respect for your own organic process. Think of the psychological growth you're inviting and supporting through a growth mindset as more of a movement *toward* growth than a Jack-and-the-beanstalk, overnight miracle.

Being patient means accepting life as it is—at least for now. It's a way of giving yourself, your partner, and your relationship credit. It helps recalibrate your monitor and adjust for unforeseen obstacles. It finds things to celebrate along the way, as you progress. Patience keeps you grounded where you are while also trusting the process to carry you where you're going.

When you have a hard time being patient, your mantra is, "I can trust life to unfold in my own best interest in its own timing." Try using this mantra when you feel impatient.

Curiosity

Choose to be curious and you will naturally cultivate a growth mindset. This is because when you're curious, you put your automatic assumptions about people, places, things, experiences, and events on hold. You're willing to experience the discomfort of not knowing in the service of learning. If you allow your own natural curiosity to arise—whether it's about internal experiences and vulnerabilities or about your partner—you invite and support discovery. When you're curious, you value learning as an end in itself. It's not just a means to an end.

If curiosity were a prescription drug, you'd see ads like this one on television, subway platforms, computer pop-ups, and highway billboards:

> *Curiozoloft instantly relieves pain and tension created by self-judgment, chronic blame, hopelessness, despair, black-and-white thinking, lack of empathy for others, and exhausting conflicts in your romantic relationships. Millions of people across the world have discovered the limitless uses of Curiozoloft to reduce a range of symptoms from mild confusion and depression to denial and destructive behaviors. The side effects are ease, energy, gratitude, and new discoveries. You have unlimited refills within you. No need to check with your doctor. Curiozoloft is already right for you.*

By staying curious as you practice SLOW, you're telling your unconscious, "Everything is okay. We can expand to include more. We're safe." You commit to the process of learning rather than to a specific, predetermined outcome. You recognize that most of the time, there's no urgency or danger in being with what's happening in the moment.

Here's a curiosity mantra you can use to cultivate a growth mindset: "Things can be interesting and valuable even if they're not what I expect." Try using this mantra when you're frustrated or bored.

Nonattachment

Although this concept tends to be associated with spiritual or religious traditions, anyone looking to connect more joyfully with their partner can benefit from practicing nonattachment. Anything we desire unfolds with less resistance, judgment, and frustration when we soften our rigid expectations of how the things we want "should" be.

When my husband and I first moved into our home a few years ago, we needed a new table for our dining room. He wanted something practical, sturdy, and affordable. I wanted something bright and elegant. After weeks of searching, repeated disagreements, and several rounds of dueling blame, control, worry, doubt, and self-pity rumination cycles, we found a table we both liked. It was farmhouse-inspired and affordable, but it still had some flair.

Shortly after it arrived, the white paint that had been used to finish it started to flake. The store sent us a replacement table.

Its finish flaked too, the same way it had with the previous one.

By the time our third replacement table arrived and the paint started flaking, we had two choices: give up and restart a grueling search for a new table that met both of our criteria or accept this table as it was, flaking paint and all.

In the end, we chose option two: accept the imperfect, flaking table. This situation nudged us into practicing nonattachment. Our perfect table didn't exist in reality. It existed only in our minds. After all the late-night internet searches and debates, after the disappointment we'd experienced with each replacement, we finally let go and accepted what we got.

We still have the table seven years later. We've come to like it as it is.

Often, the table in our relationship isn't an object or a piece of furniture. It's our expectation of how much time we'll spend with our partner one evening. It's our view of how our partner should handle themself in social situations. It could be our vision of how often we'll have sex or what good sex is. There are many immaterial things in relationships we think we want until we get them and discover they're imperfectly finished and flaking. We may send them back for a replacement. Then the replacement arrives and starts to peel and flake too.

Nonattachment isn't bland, neutral indifference. When you practice nonattachment, you're practicing receiving and appreciating what you *do* get. This isn't the same thing as selling yourself short or giving up on your goals and desires. It's more about shifting your allegiance from your idea of something (or someone) to what the thing (or person) actually is. "Only when the ones we love are no longer fantasies in our minds, do those people become real to us—then love begins" (Frederickson 2017, 132). Nonattachment is about releasing your inflexible attachment to a fantasy.

Your ability to cultivate nonattachment in SLOW sets you up to be with whatever it is your overthinking blocks. Often, when you slow down and open to your inner experiences and vulnerabilities, what you end up "getting" is a more mysterious and precious gift beyond what you could have planned or predicted. Your nonattachment mantra is: "I can learn, have, and enjoy more by relaxing my grip on the outcome I had in mind and receiving the positive in what's arriving now." Use this mantra when the things you get don't seem to live up to your expectations.

The first of the next two exercises is designed to show you areas of strength and opportunity—especially when it comes to being patient, curious, and practicing nonattachment. In the second exercise, you'll look at specific thoughts you've identified in previous rumination cycles and challenge them. These exercises can help you soften fixed beliefs as you cultivate a growth mindset.

SOLO EXERCISE: Path to SLOW Down

Use this questionnaire to highlight areas of strength and opportunity when it comes to inviting patience, curiosity, and nonattachment as you prepare to practice SLOW.

Write the numbers 1 through 12, each on its own line in a journal. As you read each item below, write the number that represents the response that feels true for you: 1 for "never," 2 for "rarely," 3 for "sometimes," 4 for "often," and 5 for "always."

When you're done, share your answers with your partner (refer to the Speaker and Listener responsibilities in the introduction for a refresher on creating safety and supporting connection). For a PDF worksheet of this exercise, go to http://www.newharbinger.com/50034.

1. I'm willing to slow down if it means I'll understand things better.

2. I openly embrace feeling bored.

3. With complex problems, I take my time discovering solutions.

4. Even when things go wrong, I'm confident I'll learn something from them.

5. Listening to others expands my perspective.

6. I'm at peace when events don't turn out the way I want them to.

7. I enjoy learning.

8. I believe in working through resentment for my own well-being.

9. I find silver linings in adversity.

10. I usually end up caring more about the process of reaching my goal than about the goal itself.

11. When I don't force life, what unfolds is often better than I expected.

12. I find challenges interesting.

Patience

Add up your scores for questions 1, 3, 9, and 11. If you scored between 16 and 20, a patience mindset may be one of your strengths. If you scored between 10 and 15, you may overcontrol outcomes and find it hard to trust progress that's not on your timeline. Keep this mantra handy: "I can trust life to unfold in my own best interest in its own timing." If you scored 9 or under, remember that change unfolds gradually. Use the "Getting Grounded in One Breath" exercise to reconnect with the here and now when you feel yourself growing impatient.

Curiosity

Add up your scores for 2, 5, 7, and 12. If you scored between 16 and 20, curiosity may be one of your strengths. If you scored between 10 and 15, you may get bored, restless, or frustrated when you try new things that don't produce the results you want fast enough. Nurture a curiosity mindset and keep this mantra handy: "Things can be interesting and valuable even if they're not what I expect." If you scored 9 or under, practice letting go of what you think you know—or what you think is worth paying attention to—and notice overlooked details.

Nonattachment

Add up your scores for 4, 6, 8, and 10. If you scored between 16 and 20, nonattachment may be one of your strengths. If you scored between 10 and 15, you may become frustrated with the results you get when they don't align with your perceived efforts. Keep this mantra handy: "I can learn, have, and enjoy more by relaxing my grip on the outcome I had in mind and receiving the positive in what's arriving now." If you scored 9 or under, practice seeing the bigger picture of situations that frustrate you as you let go of rigid expectations.

SOLO EXERCISE: Consider the Alternative

The Work is a method of inquiry created by Byron Katie (2002) to help people reduce their own suffering by investigating their most judgmental and painful thoughts so they can see what lies beyond them. Katie's The Work involves filling out a "Judge Your Neighbor Worksheet," asking four questions to investigate the truth of thoughts and who you might be without them, and finally shifting your perspective by "turning your thoughts around" (for more on The Work, go to http://www.thework.com).

In this same spirit of inquiry, we'll look at thoughts you've already written down in chapter 1. Select a couple of the blaming, worrying, doubting, controlling, or self-pitying thoughts you identified in the "Rumination Cycles Log" exercise and adjust each one in some small way—such as by changing one or more pronouns or substituting a contrasting adjective—to create an alternative version of it.

Make sure this alternative thought draws on the content of the old thought while also contradicting it in at least one detail, expressing a diverging viewpoint or offering a new perspective. You'll know you've hit gold when your first reaction is skeptical but also surprised and curious. "This can't be true—wait a minute... *Could* it?" If you can be with this skeptical reaction rather than getting caught up in defensive thinking, a softening can occur. Ask yourself, "Is any small part of this alternative thought true?" You may recall Manuel and Lisette lying in bed in chapter 1 with Manuel wanting closeness while Lisette ruminated about her mother, her body, and wanting to have a child. When Lisette begins examining her mindset, she reviews her rumination cycles and comes up with these two lists:

Labeled Thoughts	Alternative Thoughts
Manuel doesn't get me.	I don't get Manuel.
He wishes I were thinner.	He does not wish I were thinner.
He doesn't care about me.	I don't care about me.

When you've identified thoughts and provided alternative views, look over your two lists. Is there any truth to the alternative thoughts? Could any part of them be accurate?

In the examples above, Lisette might call to mind the small things Manuel does every day that show how much he cares, like preparing her dinner and encouraging her to see her mom. She might remember he regularly appreciates her kindness and celebrates the way she looks, so it doesn't make sense to believe he doesn't find her attractive or desirable. She may recognize it's been weeks since she's sent him a loving text, hugged him spontaneously, or told him she missed him, so maybe she could focus on showing him more love.

Go through this process for each ruminative thought you've written down: come up with an alternative view and see if you can be with it long enough to experience a softening. This softening may be physical as you notice tension release from your jaw, neck, or other muscles, or it may be emotional as you connect with a sense of sadness, hope, or ease. This softening can give you a taste of what it feels like to shift from a fixed to a growth mindset. For a PDF worksheet of this exercise, go to http://www.newharbin ger.com/50034.

In this chapter, you looked at how a fixed mindset reinforces viewing yourself, other people, and situations as unchanging, whereas a growth mindset helps you see opportunities and possibilities, even in difficult or unpredictable situations. You were also introduced to some of the ways that cultivating patience, curiosity, and nonattachment in a growth mindset can help you explore what lies beyond rumination cycles.

Next, you'll be introduced to the first step of SLOW: seeing.

CHAPTER 4

See Thoughts to Become Aware of Rumination Happening

A study conducted by Queens University in Kingston, Canada, suggests that the average person has around 6,200 thoughts per day—or 2,263,000 thoughts per year (Tseng and Poppenk 2020). For a couple, after a decade, we're talking roughly 4,526,000,000,000 combined thoughts.

The Queens University researchers use the descriptor "thought worms" for individual thoughts. In a simple representation of brain activity patterns, when a new thought begins, it's depicted on a graph as overlapping points. This new "worm" of brain activity has a beginning and an end. The points composing it unfold in a wormlike pattern as several seconds pass. When one pattern ends, a new activity pattern begins at a different point on the researcher's graph. This means a new thought has initiated.

As exciting as it may be for researchers in a lab to identify the worms of brain activity that constitute individual thoughts, this research won't do you much good if you remain unaware of when your own thoughts are arising and leaking out into your relationship field expressively, through toxic omissions, or energetically. This is why seeing your thoughts is the first step in reducing overthinking through SLOW. Seeing your thoughts *as thoughts* highlights what they are *not*. They are *not* the truth. They are *not* you. They are *not* your partner. They are *not* reality.

They *are* thoughts.

Eckhart Tolle (2008) puts it this way, "To see one's predicament clearly is a first step toward going beyond it" (131). In this chapter, you'll learn how to see your thoughts for what they are more often. Although I won't ask you to see all 6,200 thoughts you have daily, I will invite you to take time each day to make seeing your own thoughts a priority.

Harnessing Attention and Awareness to See

In your busy, day-to-day life, you probably juggle multiple focal points simultaneously. Chances are, you're very good at doing two or more tasks at once, like scrolling through emails and reminding your partner to pick something up at the store or half-listening to someone in the next room as you record a voice message on your phone. Multitasking—or doing several things at the same time without giving any of them your full attention—may be as old as the human mind, but with the help of technology, it has become a modern-day epidemic. Glance around at an intersection and count how many people stare at cell phones while waiting for the light to change—or worse, keep staring at cell phones when they start driving again.

Single-tasking seems to have become a precious and valuable skill, a throwback to a bygone era, like heirloom tomatoes or handwritten letters. But can we truly afford to lose the ability to single-task? Research shows multitasking takes extra time and energy because you're shifting mental gears whenever you toggle back and forth between separate tasks (Smith 2001). Directing your full attention and awareness into the nooks and crannies of your internal experiences at key moments is the opposite of multitasking. It's also how you'll be seeing thoughts in the first step of SLOW.

Visualize a flashlight beam you focus or widen with a twist of the handle. Attention is the narrower, pointed beam, and awareness is the wider, expansive beam. Whether you use attention in a point of focus or relax it into the broader focus of awareness, in order to see thoughts you'll begin by putting down your phone and your to-do list as you engage in single-tasking.

How to See Thoughts

Here are four basic steps you can use to see thoughts:

1. Pause. *Stop what you're doing for one minute.*

2. Direct your attention inward or relax into a full-bodied experience of awareness. *Notice whatever mental or cognitive activity is taking place within you in the here and now.*

3. Inquire. Ask, *"Is what's happening in my mind a thought (or a series of thoughts)?"*

4. Tune in. *Is the answer to this question yes, maybe, or no?* (If it's "no," you're probably focused, in the flow of the task, or at peace. If it's "maybe," go through steps 1 through 4 again until you receive a clear answer.)

But if I already know *I'm usually thinking,* you may be wondering, *why do I need to take time to see my own thoughts?* The reason is that theoretically knowing you're thinking isn't the same thing as being aware of thoughts as they're surfacing in the moment. By recognizing thoughts for what they are when they arise, you're harnessing active thinking. You're shining the beam of your attention and awareness on passive thoughts— the building blocks of rumination cycles.

To use another metaphor, seeing your thoughts is the equivalent of throwing flour onto ghosts. You won't really know the ghosts are there until you perceive their contours.

When you ask yourself, "Is what's happening in my mind a thought (or a series of thoughts)?" it's not just a rhetorical question. You're taking a moment to directly track your mental activity in the here and now. You're seeing what's happening in your mind as an observer rather than as a participant, and because of this, you're no longer submerged in a stream of passive thinking. Seeing your passive thoughts for what they are—thoughts—means you're coming up for air. You're ready to look at the stream of thinking in your mind as something other than absolute truth.

Make seeing thoughts a daily practice. It shouldn't take more than a minute each time you do it. In emotionally charged situations, try seeing your thoughts several times over the course of a few minutes. If your partner cancels dinner and your mind spins with thoughts like, *They're trying to hurt me intentionally. I can't trust them. Why would they do this to me? I'll show them by going out alone tonight,* seeing these thoughts as thoughts interrupts the momentum of your blame cycle. Instead of automatically believing your thoughts are accurate representations of reality simply because you're upset while they're cycling through your mind, you'll be throwing a handful of flour on your passive thinking.

Granted, seeing thoughts usually isn't all that exciting. It's like playing scales on a piano or lifting and lowering your legs as you jog the same route through your neighborhood. But the more you do it, the better you will get at it. Your ability to use attention and awareness to single-task in this way will grow. The better you get at it, the more you can use it to reroute your energy away from overthinking toward activities and capacities like *being with* what's happening in the moment and experiencing life directly.

Here are some ways to make SLOW seeing a healthy habit:

- Put sticky notes around your home that read, "Got thoughts?"

- Wear an unusual piece of jewelry that serves as a reminder to pause and see thoughts.

- Write the four steps of how to see thoughts on a mirror with an erasable marker: pause, direct attention inward, inquire, tune in.

- Take a picture of the four steps and use it as wallpaper on your phone or computer.

The more you see thoughts when the stakes are low and you're feeling calm, the easier it will be to see them when you're upset and the stakes are high. Seeing thoughts regularly will also set you up to dive deeper into labeling, step two in the SLOW process.

Warning Lights

Warning lights are indicators that something is wrong and requires your attention. Think of them as the equivalent of the fuel gauge on a car. Whether warning lights show up in bodily symptoms, behavioral signals, or feedback from your partner, they sound their own version of a high-pitched alarm, saying, "Pay attention! Something distressing is happening." When you're willing to notice warning lights, you can use them as reminders to practice seeing your thoughts and recognizing rumination cycles.

Ignoring warning lights is human. When a light flashes and the words "low fuel" pop up on a dashboard, many drivers shrug and think, *No big deal, I'll stop at a gas station later today when I have time.* If they *do* remember the warning light and fill their tank later, then the cost of ignoring it when it first started flashing will be minimal. But if a snowstorm hits on a highway and your car stalls five miles from the nearest gas station, the cost will be high.

Warning lights take two forms: personal cues and partner cues.

Personal cues are things you notice—your own nervous tics, aches and pains, rumination cycles, unwanted physical and mental health symptoms, and self-destructive or unhealthy behaviors. When aggression, stonewalling, or excessive emotionality are go-to defenses, they can also be personal cues, if you're willing to notice them and get curious about what's behind them. Apparent "bad luck" can be another personal cue, particularly if it always seems to strike when you're anxious or upset.

Partner cues, on the other hand, are things your partner picks up on about you, usually behaviors that come out or get worse when you overthink. Usually, partner cues are unconscious reactions or nervous habits you indulge in that annoy, hurt, or concern your partner. If you're in a control cycle while you and your partner are out hiking, they may experience you as micromanaging them and say "I know what I'm doing. I've been on hundreds of trails. Please stop controlling me!" In this case, your micromanaging behavior is a partner cue. If you're spinning worry and blame cycles as tax season approaches, your partner may notice that you've started judging people who you perceive as rich and undertipping waiters. Your judgmental attitude and lack of generosity are partner cues. Whenever you get caught in worry cycles about money, your partner notices these behaviors surfacing and gets annoyed with you for making assumptions and being stingy.

Seeing Personal Cues

We all have a well-being baseline when stress is low and we feel safe and content. At these times, our interactions with our partner are usually more positive. There are other times when the most basic self-care activities—like preparing a meal, taking a shower, or coordinating schedules—can drain our emotional resources. Warning lights in the form of personal cues are indicators you pick up on yourself that you've moved away from your well-being baseline.

Anxiety and tension show up in our minds and bodies in the form of thoughts, feelings, sensations, and behaviors. Personal cues can be physical tension, changes in appetite or sleep patterns, unhealthy or impulsive actions, and mood shifts. Sometimes, apparently random bad luck serves as a personal cue. Bad luck isn't always as random as it seems when your own anxiety leads you to behave in ways that increase the likelihood of mishaps and accidents.

You met Michael and Darlene in chapter 1, the night before their engagement dinner. A few months into being newlyweds, as they're preparing to go out with friends, Darlene says, "Please don't drink more than one beer tonight." Michael immediately lapses into a self-pity cycle: *What am I, a child? Everyone always tries to control my life. Nobody has any faith in me. It's not fair. I work hard. I'm a grown man. What have I done to deserve this? Why can't I drink as much as I want in my free time?*

Michael doesn't realize he tends to ruminate whenever Darlene asks him to be mindful or careful—whether it's about his alcohol use, how much he spends, or how fast he drives. But he does notice that annoying little accidents always seem to happen whenever Darlene makes this kind of request. He cuts himself shaving, he trips on his way outside, or food spills onto his dry-cleaned pants. This time, his phone slips from his hand as he's trying to arrange an Uber pickup. Luckily, when it lands against the driveway, the screen doesn't crack—this time. Because Michael has been practicing seeing his own warning lights, he knows a mishap like this is usually a personal cue for rumination. He practices getting grounded in one breath and takes a moment to pause, turn his attention inward, and see his own negative thoughts cycling.

Seeing Partner Cues

Has your partner ever asked you: "What's wrong?" Or maybe they've said in a worried voice, "Are you okay?" These questions aren't as out of the blue as they seem.

Often, our partners pick up on things we do when we ruminate that even we don't know we're doing. They observe us biting our nails as we drive, surfing the internet, and repeatedly opening the refrigerator door to stare blankly at the food on the shelves. They notice us talking too quickly, bumping into things, and cursing under our breath as we search for sunglasses propped up on our own heads. If you regularly speed up when you drive or hit the brake abruptly, your partner may recognize these reactions as a sign that you're in a blame, control, worry, doubt, or self-pity cycle. They've witnessed your warning lights plenty of times in the past, and they've seen the worst of what can happen when you overthink.

It's not easy to accept input when your threat link is active and your partner seems to be criticizing you. But there are ways to give and receive information regarding partner cues. If you notice something about your partner that may be a warning light, try saying:

- I'm noticing something you may not be aware of. Can I share?

- Something you did just now made me curious about where you are. I'd like to tell you what it was, if you're okay with that.

- I'm picking up on something. Are you willing to hear?

- I have a concern. Let me know if you're open to feedback.

- I think I noticed a warning light. Are you available to hear what it was?

If your partner says any of these things to you, do your best to respond nondefensively. Remind yourself that your partner cares about you and that their goal isn't to find fault with you—it's to nurture interdependence, healthy boundaries, and safety in your relationship.

If you *are* open and available to hear what your partner has to say, answer with, "Yes, I'm available to listen now." Then assume the Listener role and take in what your partner has to say. When your partner is done sharing, say, "Thanks for letting me know," "I appreciate you paying attention," or "I'll do my best to bring more awareness to that cue and my mental state."

If you're *not* available to listen or hear your partner's feedback, be honest about this. Don't pretend you're open when you're not in order to avoid disappointing them. Let your partner know when in the near future you might be open to listening. You might respond with:

- Thanks for checking with me. I can tell I'm not open right now. Can you ask me again later?

- I don't have the bandwidth in this moment. I'll do my best to get centered soon. Can you give me some time?

- I want to hear what you have to say at some point today, but now just isn't a good time. I'll circle back when I'm more open to taking in your feedback.

Our partners can serve as mirrors reflecting back aspects of ourselves we're often too caught up in our own thoughts to notice. They observe us from the outside, and they see past our blind spots and pick up on our warning lights at times when we can't. Their feedback is an invitation for us to recognize our overthinking.

SOLO EXERCISE: My Warning Lights List

In a journal, write "My Warning Lights List" at the top of the page. Read the lists below and write down the personal and partner cues that resonate most for you. Add any other cues you can think of that aren't on the list. Circle three cues you're committed to paying close attention to as you begin practicing SLOW. For a PDF worksheet of this exercise, go to http://www.newharbinger.com/50034.

Review this list often to increase your awareness of your own cues. Every time you discover a new personal or partner cue, add it to the list.

Personal Cues

* I have a hard time with sleep (too much, too little, being tired after sleeping).

* Parts of my body hurt for no apparent reason (jaw, neck, back, muscles, joints, head).

* I'm critical of myself and others.

* I engage in a nervous habit (picking, biting, chewing, tapping).

* I disregard my own health-related limits (such as by eating poorly, too much, or too little; overworking; disregarding my need for exercise or social connection; smoking; drinking alcohol; using or overusing mind-altering substances; gaming; excessive internet use).

* Friends, family members, my partner, and coworkers seem to be avoiding me.

* Strangers, acquaintances, and friends have been unusually critical of me.

* I forgo healthy activities I enjoy (such as spending time with friends, reading, journaling, playing an instrument, exercising, meditation, volunteer work, travel).

* I get excessively busy.

* I have more annoying accidents or bad luck than usual (for example, stubbing my toe or injuring other parts of my body; getting parking tickets; losing my cell phone, wallet, or keys).

Partner Cues

* My partner says I haven't been acting like myself lately.

* My partner gets defensive and insists I'm thoughtless.

* My partner has asked me/us to get help/see a therapist.

* My partner wishes I took better care of myself.

* My partner says I'm stressed, depressed, angry, or checked out.

* My partner says I drink or work too much or overuse my phone.

* My partner says I've been sleeping, exercising, or eating too much, too little, or poorly.

* My partner has pointed out a bad habit I've been engaging in a lot lately.

SOLO EXERCISE: Thinking About vs. Being With Cues

In a journal, at the top of a page, make three columns with these headings: "Personal/Partner Cue," "Thinking About," and "Being With." Then, identify three specific, recent incidents when a "warning light" flashed—either a personal or partner cue. Write each of these three cues down under the "Personal/Partner Cue" column.

In the "Thinking About" column, write an example of the ruminative thoughts that accompanied these cues. Finally, in the "Being With" column, imagine how you might have viewed these cues differently if you shifted from a *thinking about* to a *being with* approach.

The night before her engagement dinner, Darlene, from chapter 1, identified one of her personal cues under the "Personal/Partner Cue" as eating two pints of ice cream. Under the "Thinking About" column she wrote: "What's wrong with me? I shouldn't have eaten all that ice cream. That was such a dumb thing to do. Why can't I take better care of myself?" In the "Being With" column, she wrote, "Bingeing on sweets is one of my warning lights for rumination. I guess I'm scared my dad and my future father-in-law will make a scene."

Practice doing this for each of the three cues you've written down. To download a PDF worksheet of this exercise, go to http://www.newharbinger .com/50034.

JOINT EXERCISE: Seeing Warning Lights

Take turns asking and answering the following questions, referring to the Speaker and Listener responsibilities in the introduction for a refresher on creating safety and supporting connection.

* Can you tell when I'm engaged in negative thinking? Do you have an example?

* What do I do when I'm caught in a cycle? When I do that, what's your fear?

* Do you lapse into rumination cycles of your own when I do that?

* How do you try to help when you notice one of my warning lights? How do I typically react?

* What would be a better way for me to respond? How might that help?

Seeing Dead-End Scripts

When ruminative thoughts and warning lights go unseen, partners end up enacting dead-end scripts. Dead-end scripts are harmful, predictable ways of speaking, acting, and reacting to your partner that interfere with spontaneity, devitalize your relationship, and hold partners hostage to the past by recreating it in the present. Dead-end scripts lock you into outdated versions of yourselves that keep you stuck as a couple. When you see your dead-end script, you and your partner are in a better position to change the lines and rewrite the plot.

Schemas are limiting ways of perceiving the world and organizing information that lead to predictable, unwanted results (Young, Klosko, and Weishaar 2003). Similarly, dead-end scripts become self-fulfilling prophecies. In a dead-end script, you'll find yourself saying the same sarcastic, judgmental, or unkind things to your partner over and over again in different situations. You'll also remain on the receiving end of predictable reactions from your partner.

Below, you'll be introduced to ten dead-end scripts. Don't be surprised if several of them are familiar to you or if you've recited lines from different scripts with different partners. You may have several scripts going at once or get caught in new scripts after resolving old ones.

The more you see your script, the more you can shift into a growth mindset and get curious. Because blame and fear sustain dead-end scripts, you can learn about the buried or denied vulnerabilities that fuel them by openly and honestly sharing what you notice yourself predictably doing and saying in different scripts. When you choose to *be with* your own vulnerabilities rather than defend against them with rumination cycles, you're shifting your weight from the overused *thinking about* leg to the underdeveloped *being with* leg. You're expanding your *being with* capacity and inviting more balance into your relationship.

Here are ten common dead-end scripts and script summaries:

1. **Problem partner won't change**: If the "problem" partner would change, things would be good.

2. **Partner on a pedestal**: One person idealizes their partner. The idealized partner craves authentic connection.

3. **Worst-case scenario**: You avoid the "worst thing." It still happens.

4. **Unforgivable mistake**: One person can't forgive. The other can't make amends for their mistake.

5. **Interfering friends or family**: One partner's friends or family are too involved.

6. **Haunted romantic history**: Partners can't get out from under the shadow of a former lover.

7. **Too close and too far**: Partners trade roles: pursuing, distancing, and rarely meeting.

8. **Power struggle**: Partners compete for power, focused more on winning than cooperating.

9. **Grief postponed**: Partners avoid grief. Happiness eludes them.

10. **Everything else before love**: Partners postpone loving each other till they're less busy. Love withers.

If you find yourselves reciting the same old lines from any of these dead-end scripts, you can begin by recognizing where the plot of your love story is heading.

Problem Partner Won't Change

At the beginning of my relationship with my husband, we found ourselves regularly caught in this script (as many couples do). My husband was convinced I was the problem. If I didn't change, he couldn't stay with me. His rumination cycles fueled his side of this script.

Although he rarely told me his dark thoughts directly, his blame and judgment leaked into our relationship field. It was palpable. Family members and friends noticed it and wondered whether we were a good fit. So did I. The negative energy of my husband's rumination cycles was strong. It seemed to linger in our field even on days when I was in our apartment alone.

The same dead-end script fueled my side of the story. I was convinced *he* was the problem. I thought I could *never* stay with him—unless he changed. There were too many things wrong with him, too many intolerable personality traits, too many bad habits, which I tried unsuccessfully to ignore. Control and self-pity cycles fueled my side of the script. I sugarcoated my disapproval of him as best I could. He still sensed it, though, and it hurt him.

In reality, neither of us was the problem. The biggest problem was our rumination cycles and the ways we were avoiding facing and experiencing the vulnerable needs, feelings, and fears they masked. If we wanted a happier love story, we both needed to change.

If you're in the *Problem Partner Won't Change* script, ask yourself, "How is this thing I'm judging my partner for also a reflection of me? Do my blaming, controlling, worrying, doubting, or self-pitying thoughts feed the problem?"

Sometimes, both partners see the other person as the problem, as was the case with my husband and me. But if one partner has become convinced of their own superiority while the other person feels inadequate, then the *Problem Partner Won't Change* script morphs into another dead-end script: *Partner on a Pedestal.*

Partner on a Pedestal

There's a common misconception that loving someone means viewing them as wonderful all the time. In reality, idealizing others blocks love far more than it offers proof of love's existence. Viewing our partner as perfect swipes a filter onto them and airbrushes who they are. This implies they require filtering and airbrushing. When we refuse to see our partner's limitations and flaws and insist that they're superior, we're not doing them any favors. We're forcing them to be who we want them to be rather than who they are. Idealizing another person obscures their full humanity.

If we fear loss or abandonment based on early childhood experiences of neglect or rejection, then idealizing our partner can be a way of disconnecting from our own anger, insecurity, grief, or low self-esteem and trying to ensure we'll never be abandoned again by our perfect mate. Or we may be trying to inflate our sense of ourselves by exaggerating our partner's greatness so we can bask in the glow of their reflected light the way the moon basks in the glow of the sun. If we bolster our partner's misguided sense of themselves as better than others, it interferes with the give and take of genuine reciprocity.

Although being idealized and put on a pedestal may be intoxicating at first, in the long run, it cheats both partners of each other. The idealized partner says things like, "You don't see me as I am," "It's like you're a robot, and I'm a Stepford wife," "You don't love the real me," "Why can't you be genuine with me?" "Anger would be better than your polite façade," "I feel so alone with you." Far from enjoying their relationship field as a place of interdependence, healthy boundaries, and safety, idealized partners find themselves trapped in a golden cage.

If you're the idealizing partner in the *Partner on a Pedestal* script, spend more time being with the vulnerabilities your rumination cycles obscure. Embrace your own, and your partner's, humanity and flaws. As the idealized partner, speak up. Don't hide your flaws; acknowledge and accept them instead. Don't conspire with your partner in creating a filtered, airbrushed version of who you are. Being a living, breathing taxidermy specimen isn't everything it's cracked up to be.

The other side of idealization is devaluation. A partner who idealizes you may at some point seek to regain their fragile sense of self-confidence by devaluing you. This can shift you both into a worst-case scenario script—or one of the other dead-end scripts.

Worst-Case Scenario

You promised yourself you wouldn't have a sexless marriage, and it's been three months since you last had sex with your partner. You swore you'd never get a divorce, and your partner recently contacted a divorce attorney to "understand their rights better." You promised yourself you'd choose a partner you could rely on, the opposite of your checked-out mother, and now your beloved is working late almost every night and unavailable when you need them.

Couples caught in this script say things like, "How could they have an affair? I married them because I thought they were the opposite of my cheating father," or "All I wanted was someone to come home to. Now they work sixty hours a week, and I hardly ever see them."

Coping with an unwanted reality is painful for both partners. If the worst-case scenario happened despite one or both partners' best attempts to avoid it, spinning on rumination cycles becomes a way of avoiding facing reality and making a difficult change or choice.

If you're in the *Worst-Case Scenario* script, recognize when you're caught in anxious rumination with your partner about a situation you dread. Use the tools you've been learning to undo worry cycles. Use meditation teacher Shell Fischer's mantra: "If this thing I fear transpires the way I would like it to, that would be great. If it doesn't, that will be okay, too, because either way, I am and will be okay." Practice seeing your thoughts regularly following the steps outlined in chapter 4—pause, direct your attention inward, inquire, and tune in to yourself with awareness. Come back to experiencing your body in the present so you can *be with* your vulnerabilities instead of fueling them with overthinking.

The Unforgivable Mistake

In this script, the partner who can't forgive says, "I don't know if I'll ever forgive you. I want to, but I can't." The partner seeking forgiveness says, "I've acknowledged what happened, I've made amends, but you still won't move on. What else can I do?" Living in a state of unforgiveness torments both partners. When something has happened, it's over. It's done. It can't be altered, so ruminating about it only generates more suffering. In the words of poet Ivan Nuru (2020), "If it's out of your hands, it deserves freedom from your mind too" (39).

Do you think a lot about a mistake your partner made? Do you remind them of it? Does your partner walk around in fear of being shamed, punished, or controlled because of something they did wrong? Do they regularly apologize for what they did, deny it, or try to make up for it?

There are an infinite number of mistakes people make in relationships. There are an infinite variety of mistakes hurt partners can't forgive each other for. And there are also an infinite number of mistakes people caught in blame cycles can't forgive themselves for. If you're alive, you'll make mistakes. It's inevitable. Common lynchpins of this script are emotional and sexual affairs, debts, lies, poor decisions, and feeling abandoned at key moments (such as during an illness, when a partner loses their job, after a parent dies, or following the birth of a baby). When partners can't work toward forgiving themselves or each other for mistakes, repair becomes impossible. A relationship can't evolve without understanding, repair, and some degree of acceptance.

In the *Unforgivable Mistake* script, set the intention to repair (I'll give you additional tips on repairing in chapter 9). Practice sharing how you feel about being caught in this script using the Speaker and Listener roles. Try your best to understand your partner's take on things and the feelings they're struggling with. This can put whatever assumptions are fueling your rumination cycles into perspective. Although forgiveness can't be forced, you *can* regularly speak and listen honestly and vulnerably. When there's been a breach of trust, facing the truth with compassion reorients a couple to reality.

Interfering Friends or Family

"Your cousin should call us before showing up at our apartment!" "Why do you tell your dad all the details of our financial situation— that's not okay!" "How could you loan your college roommate our car when he still hasn't paid his last three parking tickets?" Partners with interfering family members or friends can't agree on how much access others should have to their time, energy, resources, personal information, and home. The partner who wants to establish boundaries may not understand why their partner struggles to say no to requests. The partner with the interfering family member or friend may criticize their mate for putting them in a no-win position. They believe they're being forced to "choose" between staying in the relationship or remaining on good terms with important people they love.

Sometimes, cultural differences underlie this script. If one partner's needs were secondary to the needs of their parents and siblings while the other partner grew up in an individualistic family or community, their views on appropriate boundaries with friends and family will be radically different.

If you find yourselves caught in this script, reread the section on boundary failures in chapter 2. Brainstorm ideas for setting boundaries with interfering friends and family that work for both of you. Take small steps toward nurturing interdependence, healthy boundaries, and safety in your field.

Haunted Romantic History

When a past romantic relationship persists as a feature of your current relationship, this script may be active. Like the *Interfering Friends or Family* script, couples with the anxious-avoidant ASP are primed to ruminate whenever a former spouse, boyfriend, girlfriend, or lover gets in the way of their connection. The lover in question doesn't have to be present—they may not even be in touch with them. *Rebecca*, by Daphne du Maurier (1800), is an entire novel about a fictional couple living out this dead-end script as it relates to a deceased spouse. It's usually one partner's past romantic experience that threatens their mate, setting off rumination cycles.

Doubt cycles prevail when one person questions whether their partner loves them as much as they've loved someone in the past. Blame cycles prevail when a partner in this dead-end script judges their partner's past amorous experiences. Worry cycles prevail when a person fears their mate won't stay with them. Control cycles rule whenever a person looks for evidence proving that a former lover got something precious from their partner they're not getting. This can continue even when a past lover is long gone and has no connection to a couple's current life.

Common questions and concerns in this script are: *Why did my partner date them? How could they have loved this other person and also love me when we're so different? Why is my partner obsessed with my past? Why did they choose me if they can't accept the relationships that shaped me? Is my partner with me because I'm like/unlike this former lover? Am I second best?*

Rewriting the *Haunted Romantic History* script involves recognizing rumination cycles centered around self-blame or partner-blame, feeling victimized by your partner's past (self-pity), doubting the value or importance of your relationship, controlling your partner, and worrying about the future. Explore and practice being with what lies under these cycles. In the third step of SLOW (in chapter 6), awareness anchors will support you in opening to what's happening in the moment as vulnerabilities that feed your script surface.

Too Close and Too Far

This script is the anxious-avoidant ASP playing out in its most obvious form. One partner can't get close enough while their mate can't get enough space. The partner seeking closeness may experience the partner avoiding closeness as aloof. Sometimes they believe a partner's distancing behaviors are intentionally cruel. On the other hand, the partner wanting emotional distance may experience the partner seeking closeness as dominating. It isn't unusual for this script to operate in the background while another dead-end script unfolds in the foreground, such as *Problem Partner Won't Change, Interfering Friends or Family,* and *Haunted Romantic History.*

Distance may be kept when the closeness-avoiding partner insists the closeness-seeking partner must change and meet certain criteria before love can be given. It may be enforced as one partner punishes their mate for something they did wrong. It may also be maintained through the use of other people as buffers. Interfering family, close friends, or the specters of past lovers can all act as buffers to intimacy.

In the *Too Close and Too Far* script, you can identify how you both reinforce your anxious-avoidant ASP dynamic through predictable behaviors you both engage in. Take steps to do things differently, whether this means giving your partner space or moving closer.

Power Struggle

When you're caught in this script, you've lost touch with one of the most important principles of a sustainable relationship: influence and power are shared. Maybe you're thinking, *Power has no place in healthy relationships.* If so, you're probably mistaking exploitation for power. True power is a dynamic, consensual exchange. It isn't inherently bad or dangerous. Power is the act of influencing your partner and allowing yourself to be influenced. If one person willingly leads while their mate willingly follows, these roles are chosen rather than dictated or enforced.

Power dynamics regularly go unacknowledged between couples. This is what makes them feel coercive or nonconsensual. Many factors play into power dynamics, including gender, age, race, sexual identity, ethnicity, social standing, class, and personality type. Power and privilege are often intertwined. Perceived worth and attractiveness also factor into power dynamics, along with what partners invest emotionally, or the things they do for each other, like making meals, paying bills, and caring for kids. If one partner has more power when it comes to making financial decisions, the other person will often have more power in another domain, like deciding on living arrangements or proximity to extended family. (See also the free bonus chapter, "Power and Privilege," available at http://www.newharbinger.com/50034.)

In the *Power Struggle* script, both partners dig in their heels and fight each other for control rather than negotiating or opening themselves to one another's influence. They fight about the quickest or most scenic route home. They fight about which couch will look good in the living room or which mattress will be most comfortable to sleep on. They fight about loading dishes in a dishwasher efficiently, when it's a good time to have sex, whose parents or siblings are nicer, the healthiest foods, and the ideal thermostat temperature.

The *Power Struggle* script can show up as relational extortion: *If you were more loving and thoughtful, I'd be more considerate of your needs. If you supported me more, I'd express affection toward you. If you shared your inner world with me, I'd stop flirting with the barista.* In this script, it doesn't matter *what* you're fighting about. What matters is winning the power contest at any cost—or at least not losing it.

Sharing and being flexible with power, being willing to hear one another's feedback, and taking in your partner's perspective are all relational skills you can practice in ordinary moments to rewrite this script. If you have a hard time in the Listener role, practice being present and nonjudgmental. Focus more on your partner when you listen and less on planning your rebuttal. If you have a hard time in the Speaker role, practice connecting with yourself and sharing vulnerably. You can change this script by making your decisions jointly and bringing awareness to hidden power dynamics that interfere with opening yourselves to one another's influence.

Grief Postponed

There are currents of grief underlying our happiest moments. When we gain something, we also lose something. As we celebrate our wedding day, we lose our old identity as single. We lose the fantasy that marriage will make us happy and whole. If we heal from pain we've suffered in past relationships, we lose the comfort of our old, familiar victim identity. Contrary to popular opinion, grieving is an ongoing, ordinary experience. It isn't just a rare event connected to major loss, crisis, trauma, or tragedy. Grief is woven into the fabric of our everyday lives.

For a couple, avoiding grief may be a way of rejecting reality. Grieving can be frightening. Although grief isn't "bad" or problematic in and of itself, our culture rarely honors or acknowledges its importance. Appearing strong, happy, and cheerful is viewed as a sign of status and success. This leaves most adults ill-equipped to handle and express their grief in a safe context.

Some everyday losses partners commonly avoid grieving are:

- the loss of comforting routines

- the loss of autonomy and independence

- the loss of carefree or unscheduled time together

- the loss of youth or health

- the loss of a previously reliable aspect of their physical or sexual functioning

- a miscarriage

- a job loss

- the death of a spouse or family member

- the loss of trust in each other

- the loss of the caretaker role when children move out of the home.

Couples may think the best way to deal with emotions arising from losses is to act as if they don't really matter and nothing has changed. They may double down on striving for happiness. They may exercise more, socialize more, make home improvements, take trips, get busy at work, caretake other people, or join Facebook groups, clubs, or causes. Although these responses can be healthy ways of coping, they're not substitutes for grieving. When couples postpone experiencing emotions related to loss, unprocessed grief contributes to anxiety, overthinking, and relationship rumination.

To rewrite the *Grief Postponed* script, couples need to begin acknowledging losses, whether recent or historical, and making time and space to grieve.

Everything Else Before Love

Chronic busyness is the behavioral equivalent of overthinking. Just as shifting from *thinking about* to *being with* can be hard to do in the moment, so can taking stock of what's important in the here and now. Like rumination, busyness without awareness becomes compulsive. It feeds into our self-concept: we're busy because we're important, successful, or needed. Keeping our own busyness going can overshadow the most essential aspect of our relational well-being: loving *now*.

It's easy for most of us to understand how partners can postpone grief. But why would anyone postpone loving each other when everyone wants to love and be loved?

Loving isn't a thing or a fixed state. It's not an object. You can't lock it away in a red velvet box. It requires attention and care. You wouldn't postpone watering a plant and then wonder why it withered. When you postpone loving your partner, they don't feel loved by you. It's that simple. Then, *they* don't show you love. When they don't show you love, you don't feel loved by them. And when you don't feel loved by them, it's easier to postpone showing them the love you feel. Busyness and love-postponing are self-perpetuating.

"We'll go out together and have fun when I'm less busy."

"We'll plan a vacation after I finish this project."

"We'll make time for sex when we're less overwhelmed."

"We'll go camping once we figure out the kids' daycare situation."

You'll know you're in this script if you hear yourself making excuses month after month for why you don't do the things that bring you and your partner joy and fuel your sense of connection, passion, and peace.

Partners who postpone loving each other till they're less busy in the *Everything Else Before Love* script can see the worry and control cycles that have them focused on the future instead of on the present. They can ask themselves, "What allows our relationship to thrive? How can we make time for this?" They can prioritize loving each other today over busyness.

Rewriting the Plot

If you find yourselves reciting lines from any of these dead-end scripts, the first thing to do is congratulate yourselves. You're seeing! Don't slip into a blame cycle like, *Oh, no, we're ruining our relationship. We're in a dead-end script. We've failed. We're doomed to read the same lines forever. This is terrible.* If there's any shame connected to seeing your dead-end script, acknowledge it, reread your Small Wins List, and add, "Seeing our dead-end script" to the list.

When you acknowledge that you and your partner are caught in a script, you can change it with the help of SLOW and the practices mentioned above, which can support interdependence, healthy boundaries, and safety. Even though these scripts aren't personal indictments or signs of failure, it's still your responsibility to see them playing out between you and your partner, change your lines, and rewrite the plot of your love story.

By single-tasking when you draw on attention and awareness, you can see thoughts, the first step in interrupting relationship rumination. When you see thoughts for what they are, you also see what they're not: absolute truth. Seeing thoughts reroutes energy away from overthinking toward *being with* what's happening in the moment. Personal and partner cues can act as "warning lights" reminding you to pause and notice overthinking. If you're caught in a dead-end script—one of ten negative feedback loops fueled by relationship rumination—seeing the rumination cycles fueling your harmful words and actions will go a long way toward rewriting your script.

Next, you'll learn about labeling, the second step of SLOW.

CHAPTER 5

Label the Mental Habit
or Pattern

Naming is the act of representing the world through symbols. It's one of our most potent cognitive superpowers. Researchers at Ohio State University have found a part of the brain in newborns that's prewired for words and letters. This area is called the visual word form area, or VWFA (Li et al. 2020). Naming—or labeling—is a way of using language to make sense of reality, and it seems to be hardwired into our physiology. The act of labeling our inner and outer worlds can also be a step on the path toward reducing rumination in our relationships.

In step two of SLOW, you'll label different elements of the mental habit or pattern involved in ruminative thinking. Building on what you've learned so far, you'll label hard-to-spot elements of rumination cycles that usually go unnoticed, starting with individual thoughts. Once you've labeled a sequence of thoughts, you'll distinguish between two types of thoughts—facts and pseudofacts. From there, you'll move to labeling the entire rumination cycle: Is it characterized by blame, control, worry, doubt, or self-pity? Finally, you'll practice labeling the trigger that set off your cycle and your underlying attachment fear.

Because so much of what can happen in your mind when you ruminate is hard to spot, labeling the patterns behind overthinking sheds light on what's going on for you internally. In the process of labeling, you put who you think you "should" be on hold as you examine who you actually are. By interrupting your habit of turning away from negative, harmful thoughts, you pull back the curtain on your vulnerabilities. Just like in *The Wizard of Oz*, once you see thoughts as they are, they lose quite a bit of their power. Even when thoughts are hard to see, labeling can help you see them a little at a time. The more you see and label thoughts, the less personally you take them.

When you disengage from ruminative thoughts, you can make new choices that shift how you think, and how much.

Record Ruminating Thoughts

The best way to record ruminative thinking is to keep a thought journal. You may want to schedule specific times during the day to stop what you're doing and see thoughts. You can program reminders into your phone: when the alert goes off, check in with what you're thinking. You can also take random samples of your thoughts throughout the day, pausing to notice any thoughts in the moment. When you capture thoughts without planning to capture them, you won't be tempted to pull the wool over your own eyes by thinking socially acceptable thoughts.

Make a point of consistently pausing whatever you're doing, seeing your thoughts, and labeling them by jotting them down. If the alert you've programmed into your phone goes off and you realize you were anxiously envisioning yourself and your girlfriend bored and miserable twenty years from now in the same small apartment you live in now, the following words might capture these thoughts: *My girlfriend won't ever travel with me and explore new places. Life is passing us by. We'll end up old and unsatisfied.*

Thoughts may arise in the form of memories, images, convictions, judgments, sensations, flashes of intuition, feelings, or a combination of these things. Because thoughts are elusive and insubstantial compared to physical objects, capturing them in language is one way of making them more static and concrete. It helps bring them into view.

Seeing and labeling thoughts accurately is a powerful stand-alone practice, regardless of what you choose to do next. Doing this can snap you out of moments of unconscious cognitive fusion, when you're so caught up in overthinking that you mistake your thoughts for reality.

Here are a few tips for labeling thoughts effectively. The more vulnerably, succinctly, and directly you use language to label thoughts, the more you can *be with* your inner experiences rather than keeping your distance from them or avoiding them with overthinking.

Use Vulnerable Language

Labeling thoughts in rumination cycles is like capturing chameleons. Passive thoughts camouflage themselves and blend into the background. Once you express them in words, it's harder for thoughts to shape-shift and elude you. You can see their true colors.

Whenever you label thoughts by writing them down, use words that reveal rather than hide. Be specific. Resist the temptation to water down or embellish your thoughts. If the words you choose are simple and emotionally resonant, you're probably labeling with accuracy.

Images of failing out of school, snippets of phrases you've heard for years about the importance of college, and memories of anxiety-provoking conversations with a partner might translate into the following sequence of labeled thoughts: *It would be really bad if I chose the wrong school. What if I fail? I'm scared this relationship won't last.*

Less Is More

As an English literature major with a history of using too many words in situations that require speaking or writing, I can relate to people who find it hard to write concisely. It has taken me a long time to understand the value of two- and three-syllable words and short sentences. When you recognize the core meaning at the heart of your thoughts—and express it succinctly—you can stop hiding what you're thinking from yourself.

Use short phrases and sentences to express each thought. Keep sentences between three and seven words. Write the way a six-year-old might speak: *I don't like her. I'm sad. It isn't fair. I want them to pay attention to me.*

Keep It Raw

If your thoughts are filled with blame, anger, self-pity, or resentment, don't be afraid to capture these emotional realities in words. The whole purpose of labeling thoughts is to see them and know them. Don't judge them—capture them instead. If you're being judgmental, capture your judgments and assumptions. Don't worry about being nice or appropriate. Be real.

Writing out your socially unacceptable thoughts has benefits. Rumination feeds on the ways we pity ourselves passively and quietly, make assumptions in secret, and stoke judgments and expectations we've never admitted to ourselves or revealed to our partners. The more "shameless" you are in translating the building blocks of overthinking into raw, honest language that you then face and recognize, the more quickly you can defuse rumination.

Test the emotional honesty of thoughts you've written down by reading them back to yourself out loud. If you sense a shift in your body as you reread your words (an emerging warmth or heat, tension in your back or jaw, a shiver, queasiness or discomfort in the pit of your stomach), you've likely touched on something true in the labeling process.

SOLO EXERCISE: Labeling My Thoughts

Set a timer (a phone alert works well) to go off once every hour for three or four consecutive hours. Every time the alert sounds, take out your journal. Avoid multitasking. Instead, focus your full attention inward. Bring awareness to the thoughts you notice when the alert sounds and write them down in short sentences, using vulnerable language, and keeping it raw. Note the time of the alert beside each thought or thought sequence.

Fact vs. Pseudofact

Your thoughts are symbolic versions of reality. They're meanings you weave around yourself, your partner, your relationship, and your life.

Once you've labeled a thought in your journal, it can no longer blend in with the background or vanish into thin air the way it might have if you hadn't labeled it. You've pinned it down—in language. Now, it's time to examine it. What does it mean? Is it worth believing? Does it contain important information? Is it spreading falsehoods? Take a look at the following labeled thoughts: *My girlfriend won't ever travel with me and explore new places. Life is passing us by. We'll end up old and unsatisfied.* Notice how the thoughts represent a constellation of assumptions and fear-based predictions about an imaginary future your mind has selected out of many different possible future outcomes related to your girlfriend, traveling, and living a fulfilling life.

When you label a thought as a fact or a pseudofact, you're sifting through the wheat and chaff of your own thinking. You're examining which of your own labeled thoughts hold some truth and which are fanciful theories. Sorting labeled thoughts into these two broad categories cuts through confusion when it comes to getting carried away on the dangerous ride of overthinking.

Facts

Facts are truths, supported by evidence. Opinions and declarations can become facts if they're proven. "The sky is blue" can be an opinion. Because blue light in sunlight bounces off atmospheric gases and particles more than the other colors in light beams due to its shorter wavelength, you may be able to support this claim with evidence. At the same time, the sky isn't always blue. Sometimes, it's red, pink, grey, and yellow. If you're color-blind, "The sky is blue" may not be a fact for you, but evidence can help you understand why it's a fact for others.

"You're happy" can be either a fact or a pseudofact about your partner. If they check in with themselves; notice an embodied, warm, expansive flow of energy making them smile, laugh, or relax; and agree with your assessment of their emotional state, you have evidence. In this case, the declaration "You're happy!" transitions from being an opinion into being a fact.

Judgments—particularly harsh or negative ones—are pseudofacts. They imply that a person, place, thing, creative idea, perspective, or value is unworthy of care, curiosity, dignity, understanding, or respect. For this reason, judgments can't be true.

Opinions and declarations are pseudofacts waiting in line to be elevated to fact status once you provide supporting evidence. If you think, *My couch will easily fit through the front door of my boyfriend's apartment*, it's an opinion until you properly measure the couch and your boyfriend's front door. Opinions and declarations aren't always rooted in disapproval the way judgments are. But they're not facts either until you support them with evidence.

Remember William and Theo from chapter 1? William ruminates about being unemployed. He thinks, *I can't live on my savings forever.* If he has $10,000 in his savings account, pays $2,000 rent for the apartment he shares with Theo and spends $800 a month on food and $500 on other expenses, then the thought, *I can't live on my savings forever,* is indeed a fact. William's other thoughts, such as *I should have done something else with my life, I'll end up homeless,* or *Theo is going to leave me,* are opinions passing as pseudofacts.

Pseudofacts

Pseudofacts are opinions, judgments, assumptions, or expectations you mistake as truths.

It's natural to judge everything from the taste of your morning coffee to how well your partner is driving. Our ability to judge allows us to be efficient in our decision making. We strive to conserve as much of our energy as we can to achieve goals and manage complex lives. This involves making split-second judgments. Judging helps us use past experiences to assess something in the present that we don't fully understand in order to accomplish a goal. At the same time, it protects us from experiencing the insecurity and anxiety we can feel when faced with the unknown.

The subtext of a negative judgment is *This person, place, thing, creative idea, perspective, or value is unworthy of care, curiosity, dignity, understanding, or respect.* Judgments offer a partial and incorrect view. When we judge ourselves or our partners, we're shrinking reality to fit this view. This may feel safer than remaining open to a more complete view. In preventing our love, respect, and care from reaching what we judge, we try to distance ourselves from our vulnerabilities.

William distinguishes between these two categories of thoughts in his rumination cycles. He recognizes *I'm a loser* and *I'm no good* as examples of judgments disguised as pseudofacts. They're partial *and* incorrect views of himself rooted in disapproval.

Similar to judgments, opinions can also be harmful in rumination cycles when they masquerade as pseudofacts and negatively impact your relationship field, your decisions, and your behaviors toward your partner. Some opinions functioning as pseudofacts in William's rumination cycle are: *It's impossible to find work at my age. I can't ask my colleagues for help. I'm doomed. I should have done something else with my life. I'll end up homeless.*

In a hodgepodge of judgments, opinions, and expectations, the thoughts spinning in your rumination cycles can look like facts when they're actually pseudofacts unsupported by evidence. Going through the process of seeing thoughts, writing them down, and labeling them as facts or pseudofacts will help you recognize the difference. This is an important process to engage in consciously and intentionally, especially when you're basing actions, choices, and decisions that impact your partner and your relationship on the 6,200 thoughts you're quietly thinking—and possibly overthinking—all day long, every day.

SOLO EXERCISE: Labeling Facts and Pseudofacts

Look through your journal and select an exercise you've already completed—one where you've labeled thoughts. For example, in the "Thinking About vs. Being With Cues" exercise, review the thoughts you wrote down in the middle column under "Thinking About." Then, create two new columns titled "Fact or Pseudofact" and "Evidence."

Note whether the thought you've labeled is a fact or pseudofact by writing "F" or "PF" beside it. If you've labeled a thought a fact, jot down the evidence you have supporting its fact status in this column. Otherwise, label whether it's a judgment, opinion, assumption, or expectation. Vince (from chapter 2) has labeled the following thoughts in his "Thinking About" column: "Ronald eats poorly," "He has high blood pressure," and "He'd take care of himself if he loved me." He labels the first and second thoughts "F" for fact, and the third thought "PF" for pseudofact. In the "Evidence" column, he writes, "I see him eat only processed food all day" to support the "F" and "Medical tests prove this" for the first and second thoughts. For the third thought, there's no hard and fast evidence; he writes, "Assumption" in the "Evidence" column.

For a PDF worksheet of this exercise, go to http://www.newharbinger .com/50034.

Label the Rumination Cycle

You can increase your understanding of the negative charge fueling your overthinking—and defuse it—by labeling your rumination cycle. As soon as you notice your mind racing, practice the first two steps of SLOW: seeing and labeling. Racing thoughts can be a personal cue for overthinking—one you can add to the Warning Lights List you created in chapter 4.

Once you've seen your thoughts, label a couple of them in your thought journal by writing them down. Recognize whether they're facts or pseudofacts. Rather than staying at the surface level of these thoughts, can you sense their emotional charge? Tap into what's fueling a sequence of thoughts you've labeled by asking yourself the following question: "Do these thoughts reflect blame, worry, doubt, control, or self-pity?" It's easier to disengage from the content of thoughts when you stop taking them at face value and consider what may be fueling them.

Labeling your rumination cycle can shift you out of mindless over-thinking into *being with* a fuller experience of what's happening within you beyond the content of thoughts.

Label the Trigger

The phrase "getting triggered" encapsulates a complex process. When you're triggered, something outside of you sets off an internal experience of threat.

Let's say you notice a red stain on your partner's shirt when he returns from a trip. The stain could be lipstick or a smear of raspberry jam. The external trigger (a red stain) connects with internal experiences (in this case, a fear of abandonment, loss, or betrayal) through an activated threat link. Very quickly, you've defended against your internal experiences with ruminative thoughts that give you an illusion of control, however painful these thoughts may be. *It must be lipstick. Oh, God, I knew this would happen sooner or later. He's having an affair. I shouldn't have trusted him. He doesn't love me. Maybe he never loved me.* Though these thoughts generate their own brand of anxiety and emotional pain, thinking them also erects a buffer of thoughts between you, your body, and your emotions.

If you interpret the red stain as raspberry jam, on the other hand, the external trigger hasn't changed. It's exactly the same. But because you've interpreted it differently, it doesn't activate the threat link. Your vulnerabilities related to fear of abandonment and betrayal remain dormant. Ruminative thoughts aren't set into motion and rumination cycles don't spin.

A trigger can be an action your partner takes—or doesn't take. Consider the long pause—an eternity!—when you say "I love you" and wait for them to say something. Or maybe you notice your partner wincing when you ask how you look in your bagel-print Hawaiian shirt. Or you smell alcohol on their breath when they kiss you goodnight and a few weeks ago they swore off drinking. Part of what makes triggers powerful is that they aren't just connected to something you experience in the present moment. They can fire up your entire unconscious attachment system. This is why they're such a big deal in relationships.

Because they're emotionally loaded, we often try to forget about triggers as quickly as possible after we've experienced them, hoping they were a one-time thing and won't return to bother us again. But they always do. Ignoring, forgetting, or minimizing triggers is part of what keeps them active—and what keeps us reactive each time they blindside us.

Labeling your triggers increases your awareness of the types of things, events, activities, situations, and people that set off your ruminative thinking in your relationship field. Knowing your triggers can help you focus on what you need in order to feel safe. Sharing your triggers with your partner can also help you collaborate to keep the peace. Although your partner isn't under any obligation to cater to all your safety needs, knowing what your triggers are provides them with important information about you.

If it triggers you when they don't call you and you feel safer when they call you a few times a day, it's not your partner's responsibility to call you regularly. At the same time, your partner may feel more inclined to reach out to you and touch base if they understand your trigger. Knowing, labeling, and accepting your hot-button triggers can move you toward relinquishing rumination as a go-to reaction when a trigger activates your threat link.

In the next exercise, you'll have an opportunity to create a Triggers List by tracking moments throughout the day when you feel overwhelmed, anxious, or uncomfortable in your relationship. Because triggers are like the claps of thunder that precede stormy rumination cycles, knowing them can alert you to an unexpected shift in your own internal weather patterns.

SOLO EXERCISE: My Triggers List

Create three columns in your journal: "Date and Time," "Trigger," and "Intensity (1–5)." When something upsetting happens, pay attention to it. If your girlfriend walks into the house ahead of you and lets the storm door fall back against you, take some time to calm down. Identify the moment that set you off and summarize it. For example, you might write, "When my girlfriend let the storm door fall back instead of holding it open" under the "Trigger" column, "Monday, 2:15" in the "Date and Time" column, and the number "3" for "moderately upsetting" in the "Intensity" column.

Repeat this process several times a day over the course of the next week until you have a list of recurring relationship triggers. When any of these triggers resurface, you'll know that your threat link may be active.

To download the PDF worksheet of this exercise, go to http://www.new harbinger.com/50034.

Labeling Attachment Fears

Individual triggers usually fall under broad categories of lifelong anxieties known as attachment fears. If you've begun creating a triggers list, you may have already noticed that even when your individual triggers vary, certain themes pop up again and again.

Attachment fears are rooted in childhood. As we explored in chapter 2, early interpersonal experiences with caregivers and authority figures you trusted or depended on to meet your physical and emotional needs have shaped your attachment style. You may have a number of attachment fears, such as being controlled, abandoned, or devalued. Any of these fears can get activated with your partner on different occasions and in different ways.

If being judged is one of your attachment fears, your partner's comment about how your dress used to fit before the holidays might activate it. A week later, this same fear might surface when they suggest you don't know what you're talking about during a heated conversation about digital nomads. Or you might experience this fear when your partner seems to be criticizing one of your friends. In each of these situations, although the trigger is different, the attachment fear is the same.

When you label ruminative thoughts, you're already starting to bring awareness to your attachment fears. Ask yourself, "What's the fear underlying these thoughts? Am I afraid of being abandoned? Trapped? Am I scared of being devalued? Do I dread being controlled?"

Attachment fears can range from the fear of being laughed at to the fear of being annihilated. Some common attachment fears are:

being abandoned	being shamed	being misinterpreted
being controlled	being tricked	being unappreciated
being rejected	being betrayed	being hurt
being violated	being laughed at	being manipulated
being unwanted	being dismissed	being objectified
being excluded	being overlooked	being used
being devalued	being unheard	being blamed
being neglected	being unseen	being targeted
being ignored	being exploited	being undermined
being mocked	being dominated	being belittled
being ridiculed	being misunderstood	being forgotten

When Kerri catches Margo FaceTiming her attractive colleague in the middle of the night, Margo is remorseful. She admits that what started out as an innocent flirtation had turned into an emotional affair. Despite Margo's commitment to regain Kerri's trust and work on herself, Kerri ruminates about Margo's colleague all the time. *What if I hadn't caught her? Would it have turned into a full-blown affair? What if she's staying with me out of guilt? What if Margo leaves me?* Kerri's work performance worsens as a result of her anxiety.

She chooses a day when she has a light work schedule and sets a timer on her phone to go off hourly between 10:00 a.m. and 4:00 p.m. When the timer buzzes, she takes two minutes to label her thoughts, distinguish between facts and pseudofacts, and label her rumination cycles, triggers, and attachment fears. If she doesn't know how to label something, she indicates this with a question mark.

For example, at 10:00 a.m., she has these thoughts: *She's going to cheat on me. I can't believe I trusted her. I'm a doormat.* Kerri marks all as "PF" for pseudofact and notes that these thoughts are spinning in self-pity and worry cycles. She also notes the trigger and writes, "A new intern at work reminded me of Margo's work colleague." Kerri recognizes her attachment fear as "being abandoned."

Acknowledging attachment fears can deepen self-compassion. Accepting attachment fears as natural and understandable is one way of embracing your humanity. These fears will be a constant across a variety of different triggers. When you take time to see and label them, you're being with them rather than defending against them with overthinking.

SOLO EXERCISE: Labeling Attachment Fears

Which fears do you experience in your relationship with your partner? Look through the attachment fears listed above or go to http://www.newharbinger.com/50034 for a PDF worksheet of this exercise. In a journal, write down three attachment fears you struggle with most—the ones that fuel recurring disagreements and conflicts.

As you go about your day and interact with your partner, keep these fears in mind. If something upsets you, check in with yourself to see if one of these fears is active. If so, label it. For example, if one of your top three attachment fears is "being ignored" and your partner continues telling you an anecdote about work even when you've asked them to stop, label your fear by acknowledging it the moment you become aware of it. You can do this by saying to yourself, "I'm experiencing my attachment fear of being ignored right now." Familiarize yourself with what this fear feels like in your body when it's active rather than thinking about how insensitive or rude your partner is, how unsure you are about the sustainability of your relationship, or how you should teach your partner a lesson. You can also restate your request and follow through with a "healthy ultimatum" like the ones discussed in the "Healthy Boundaries" section of chapter 2. This might sound like, "If you continue telling me this anecdote even though I've asked you to stop, I will leave the room."

Being with attachment fears rather than *thinking about* the situations that activate them can reduce rumination over time and increase self-awareness.

SOLO EXERCISE: Labeling Worksheet

In a journal, make six columns at the top of a page: "Time," "Thoughts," "Type," "Cycle," "Trigger," and "Attachment Fear." Then, set a timer at regular intervals to alert you to check in with your thoughts throughout the day.

When the alarm sounds, write the time in the "Time" column. Label the thoughts briefly in the "Thoughts" column, letting the content be raw and using short phrases and feeling words. Label the type of thought (fact or pseudofact) in the "Type" column. Label the type of rumination cycle in the "Cycle" column and include a brief description of a possible trigger in the "Trigger" column. Finally, label the fear you experienced in the "Attachment Fear" column. If you're not sure of what to write in any of these columns, write a question mark, N/A for "not applicable," or leave it blank.

For the PDF worksheet version of this exercise and an example of Kerri's labeling worksheet, go to http://www.newharbinger.com/50034.

If you see and label the mental habits and cognitive patterns you normally overlook, they will become aspects of your inner life to face rather than avoid. When you label and understand the attachment fears behind your triggers, you make sense of your emotional reactions. As you choose to *be with* parts of yourself you're uncomfortable experiencing and usually avoid, rumination weakens as a go-to defense.

Naming—or labeling—can be a step on the path toward reducing relationship rumination. In this chapter, you practiced using vulnerable language and brief, raw descriptions as you labelled thoughts. You also critically examined the accuracy of ruminative thoughts by assessing whether thoughts are facts or pseudofacts. Finally, you explored the connections between thoughts, rumination cycles, triggers, and attachment fears. Next, in the third step of SLOW, you'll practice opening.

CHAPTER 6

Open to What's Going On in the Moment

The present moment is where our life always unfolds. Although human beings have many ways to sidestep uncomfortable experiences in the here and now, the present encompasses all there is all the time. Our thoughts about the past happen in the present. The same goes for our thoughts about the future. And we are all connected to the present moment through the conduit of our bodies. Life always unfolds through our bodies in the here and now.

Opening takes practice. In this chapter, which focuses on the third step of SLOW, you'll be introduced to three ways you can open to what's going on within you and your relationship field: through sensations, emotions, and impulses. You'll also be introduced to four practical awareness anchors you can use anywhere, anytime to support opening. These anchors are the breath, sensations, sounds, and awareness itself.

Awareness anchors foster a more open state of mind. Use them regularly and you'll find yourself living more in the here and now than in the past or the future. Doing this can prepare you to practice opening as you connect with your vulnerabilities in SLOW. If you make opening a regular practice when you're calm and the stakes are low, it will be easier for you to draw on this ability when you find yourself reacting to a trigger or caught in a rumination cycle.

JOINT EXERCISE: Past, Present, or Future

My husband and I have a simple, four-word question we ask one another to help us return to the present moment. We might be driving somewhere, crossing a street, at dinner with friends, or passing each other in the kitchen or hallway. The question is a cue for us to pause and notice where we are in our own minds. At any moment, either of us asks: "Past, present, or future?"

If I'm the one asking, my husband might say, "Past. I was thinking about a friend's wedding." I might tell him where my mind was right before I asked him the question. For example, I might say, "Future. I was thinking about my schedule tomorrow."

Try asking one another this four-word question a couple of times a day over the course of the next week: "Past, present, or future?" Each time either of you asks, direct your attention inward for a few seconds, notice your thoughts, and answer the question honestly. Alternatively, if you're practicing on your own, set an alert to remind you to ask yourself this question.

Once you know which timeframe you're in, it's easier to remember where you actually are in this moment and to make the choice to come back to the here and now.

Vulnerability

Opening to life is an inherently vulnerable experience. At best, plugging in to the here and now brings us into direct contact with ourselves, other people, and our environment. At worst, it exposes us to discomfort, shame, anxiety, humiliation, and pain. Reverend Angel Kyodo Williams says, "In the now, we experience pain, but when we carry the pain into the next moment, then we're suffering" (Howes 2021). As part of growing up in a complicated, unpredictable world, we learn to associate being present with vulnerability and vulnerability with danger. We develop avoidance strategies to protect ourselves against direct experience.

Overthinking is our handiest and most socially acceptable vulnerability avoidance strategy. It's also how we carry our pain into the next moment and turn it into suffering. Often, the lower our tolerance level for vulnerability in a committed, romantic relationship, the more rumination follows a trigger. A threat link gets activated and our rumination kicks into gear in an attempt to reduce discomfort. Whether we're experiencing anger, love, helplessness, anxiety, unworthiness, insecurity, or a mix of these emotions, relationship rumination diverts us away from ourselves. Psychotherapist Mark Epstein (2013) puts it like this in *Thoughts Without a Thinker*: It is our fear of experiencing ourselves directly that creates suffering. Rumination is a symptom of the allergy we've developed to the present moment—and to our own vulnerability.

Author and researcher Brené Brown (2012) defines vulnerability as "uncertainty, risk, and emotional exposure." She describes it as "Waking up every day and loving someone who may or may not love us back, whose safety we can't ensure, who may stay in our lives or may leave without a moment's notice, who may be loyal to the day they die or betray us tomorrow" (34).

Sometimes we mistake emotionality or impulsivity for vulnerability. If you cry at the drop of a hat, you may think, *I know how to feel my sadness.* But what if crying is how you learned to cover up anger with tears? If you yell at your partner, you may excuse this behavior, saying, "I'm emotionally expressive." But what if yelling is how you discharge emotion without fully experiencing or connecting with it?

Allergic reactions can be reduced through immunotherapy, where exposure increases your tolerance of the "allergen" and decreases the intensity of your allergic response. Relationship rumination can also be reduced through gradual, controlled exposure to the allergen, which in this case is also the "cure:" *being with* what's going on within you in the moment.

When you open yourself to experiencing what's happening inside you, what you're doing is a form of therapeutic exposure work. In exposure work, you overcome a fear of something by being with what you fear and doing the feared activity. If you're afraid of driving over bridges, for example, you find a pedestrian walkway above a street and walk over it. If you're afraid of getting on a crowded elevator, you get on an elevator with your partner and go up a single floor. Gradually, a little at a time, you build up to driving over bridges and being on crowded elevators moving to the highest floors of tall buildings. We do therapeutic exposure work with our own vulnerability by being with what's happening in the moment when something sets us off, even when it's uncomfortable. We catch our rumination and open ourselves up to knowing and experiencing what we might not be fully aware of within ourselves.

Over time and with practice, you'll learn to trust that you can be with what's happening in the moment rather than tripping the circuit breaker of rumination. Through repeated direct experiences, you develop more trust and confidence that experiencing your vulnerability isn't inherently bad, dangerous, or intolerable.

Vulnerability Trio: Sensations, Emotions, and Impulses

The Dolby surround sound experience of our vulnerable sensations, emotions, and impulses is unpredictable, just like the world around us. Our sensations, emotions, and impulses come and go in response to the interface between our inner worlds and our external environments. They can range from very pleasant to very painful. Although we can't control the fact that they arise, we can—and do—titrate how much or how little we directly experience them.

It would be impractical and unsustainable to always connect with your sensations, emotions, and impulses. It's not helpful to open to the depths of your grief at your mother-in-law's art show just because you're feeling sad. But you *can* practice opening yourself up to grief and to the impulse to mourn in a safe way when it's appropriate. When rumination becomes your default reaction to activated threat links and relationship triggers, it cuts you off from your life, your partner, and yourself. The more authentic your relationship with yourself, the more likely you are to nurture authenticity with your partner.

In order to open yourself up to what's going on within you in the here and now, you make the choice to regularly *be with* your own sensations, emotions, and impulses.

Opening to Sensations

Sensations and the body are interconnected. Being fully alive means seeing, smelling, tasting, touching, and hearing. Opening to sensations means allowing yourself to experience life through your senses. Remember the flashlight from chapter 5? As you relax the beam of your awareness into a broad, expansive focus that includes your body, you gain access to sensations of all kinds.

It's not that hard for us to mute or block the data our senses transmit. It's common to prioritize our thoughts and impulses over sensations. For many of us, strength, competence, productivity, and intelligence are all-important. We've learned these are the nonnegotiable qualities, skills, and capacities that will allow us to stay safe, succeed, and thrive. Sometimes, we've suffered a trauma that has made it hard for us to trust our own bodies. Trauma can leave us dissociated from our bodies as a protection against future violations.

The warmth of a hug, a paper cut, the tang of raspberries—these are all sensations. Physical pleasure and physical pain encompass a wide range of sensations. If you block experiences available to you in this area of your inner life, you short-circuit your own access to the scope and breadth of intelligence in your body.

When rumination inhibits awareness of sensations, practice opening by asking yourself, "What sensations am I aware of in my body right now?" Then, stay tuned in to your body and notice what arises. Be patient and curious. Practice nonattachment.

Opening to Emotions

Paul Eckman (2007) asserts there are six basic emotions: happiness, sadness, fear, disgust, anger, and surprise. In his view, all other emotions are a combination of these. A recent study in *PNAS* published in 2017 sets forth twenty-seven distinct core emotions: admiration, adoration, aesthetic appreciation, amusement, anger, anxiety, awe, awkwardness, boredom, calmness, confusion, craving, disgust, empathic pain, entrancement, envy, excitement, fear, horror, interest, joy, nostalgia, relief, romance, sadness, satisfaction, sexual desire, and surprise (Cowen and Keltner 2017). Opening to emotions means getting to know your own emotions by experiencing them more deeply and fully when they arise.

By avoiding—or controlling—unwanted emotions, you reduce your direct experience of them. Nevertheless, emotions continue surging through you. Sometimes, you've blocked them so well you're not aware of them. Like the cell phone you pull out of your back pocket to avoid feeling lonely when your partner plays video games, the ice cream you eat to numb anxiety, or the credit card or vape cartridge you reach for to distract yourself from feelings of insecurity, rumination becomes automatic. It's a distraction from loneliness, sadness, helplessness, and other emotions. But these uncomfortable experiences don't vanish when you block them. They're still in you—muted and hidden under layers of tension and overthinking.

Opening to what's present for you emotionally can reconnect you with your true needs. If relationship rumination has blocked your emotional life, draw on a growth mindset and practice opening. Ask yourself, "What's here emotionally right now?" Tune in to any emotional undercurrents within you and notice what arises.

Opening to Impulses

Impulses are the seeds of actions before they've been converted into behaviors. They precede actions as urges, wants, needs, and desires.

All actions and behaviors start with an impulse, but not all impulses end in behaviors and actions. You can be aware of your impulses without acting on them. You can also be unaware of your impulses while you *do* act on them. Opening to impulses means letting yourself *be with* the experience of your own impulses. Then, you decide whether or not to act on them—and *how*. Even if you don't act on an impulse, opening to it and knowing it can serve you. Impulses contain valuable information. They intersect and overlap with sensations and emotions in a rich, interdisciplinary dialogue.

Opening to and understanding your own impulses supports healthy thinking, decision making, and problem solving. Impulses, like emotions, aren't good or bad. They're information in the form of raw embodied experience. When you open to impulses, you look at what's driving you under the surface. You get curious about your reactions. Is there an impulse to constrict, move toward your partner, or turn away? In a moment of anger, does energy surge into your legs and arms? When your partner criticizes you, does something go limp within you, like a wooden finger puppet?

If rumination blocks your impulses—or you regularly act on impulses without understanding what you're doing and why—practice opening. Ask yourself, "Can I notice my experience of this impulse in my body and choose to *be with it* rather than act on it? What's this impulse telling me?" Tune in to impulses within you patiently and with curiosity, letting go of any outcome you're hoping for or dreading. Notice what arises.

JOINT EXERCISE: Vulnerability Trio Quiz

Because our partners are on the receiving end of our defenses—such as rumination—they can be better at intuiting our vulnerabilities than we are. This is why you'll answer the following questions about *one another* rather than about yourselves.

If you're taking this quiz alone, you can still complete it. Answer the questions about yourself rather than your partner as objectively as possible, the way someone might who knows you well.

In a journal, write the numbers 1 through 9, with each number on its own line. Write your response to each quiz question on its corresponding line.

If you're taking this quiz with a partner, go over one another's answers in the Speaker and Listener roles. Don't try to analyze one another or prove anything based on your answers. The purpose of this quiz is to increase awareness of your vulnerabilities. To download a PDF version, go to http://www.newharbinger.com/50034.

1. I think my partner is tuned in *most* to sensory experiences related to:

    a. sights

    b. smells

    c.   tastes

    d.   touch/physical sensations

    e.   sound

2. One example of a time when my partner seemed tuned in to what I circled in the last question is: _____.

3. (True/False) I've noticed my partner tends to wait till the last minute to eat, sleep, use the restroom, or take care of an injury.

4. I would rate my partner's comfort level experiencing the full range of their emotions as:

    a.   total ease

    b.   mostly easeful

    c.   some unease

    d.   uneasy

    e.   very uneasy

5. (True/False) Under the right circumstances, my partner can calmly and directly talk about it when they're angry, sad, vulnerable, scared, lonely, or jealous.

6. (True/False) There are certain emotions or feelings my partner is more comfortable with (for example, anger or joy) and others they're less comfortable with (for example, fear or sadness).

7. (True/False) My partner is able to be spontaneous and also appropriately cautious, depending on the situation.

8. My partner is best at (choose one):

    a.   soothing themselves

    b.   choosing the right moment to say tough things

    c.   receiving feedback nonreactively

9. My partner sometimes has a hard time:

    a.   making decisions

    b.   taking necessary risks

    c. setting appropriate boundaries in the heat of the moment

Questions 1 through 3 reference sensory life. Questions 4 through 6 reference emotional life. Questions 7 through 9 reference impulses.

Whether you took this quiz alone or with a partner, use it to help you recognize where you may struggle with the "vulnerability trio" in relationships. If you tend to block sensations, reread the "Opening to Sensations" section in this chapter and practice tuning in to your sensations every day. If you tend to block your own emotions, reread "Opening to Emotions" and get curious about the emotional undercurrents running below the surface of your interactions. If you tend to suppress impulses, reread the section on "Opening to Impulses" and tune in to your impulses instead of ignoring them or acting on them.

Scanning and Anticipating

As your partner walks beside you, you wonder, *Will they take my hand? Are they thinking about something else—or someone else? Do they care? Should I introduce the topic of how I feel about living together now, or will they pull away from me and shut down if I do?*

Your partner said they'd be home in twenty minutes. It's been half an hour. *Did they forget our agreement? Did they get in an accident? What's taking them so long? I hope they're not caught in traffic. They could at least text me. Why can't they be more considerate?*

You hear a loud exclamation followed by a string of curses in the next room. *Oh, no. Did they bump into a piece of furniture? What happened, and how will it affect their mood? It's hard living like this, never knowing when they'll get mad or upset. I'm always walking on eggshells. I wish they'd be happier and more mindful. I wish they'd control their frustration better.*

Your nervous system constantly scans its surroundings. Its job is to figure out if you can relax. It's as if you have invisible antennae extending out into your relationship field, picking up on different frequencies and energies. Whether you realize it or not, you are constantly scanning your environment for dangers you've survived and making assessments about whether those past dangers are resurfacing in the present. "We are always in a constant state of environmental assessment, assigning meaning to all perceptual experience, dealing with unknowns, reducing uncertainty, and maintaining the balance between learning new information and adhering to previously learned understandings," writes Tim Hicks (2018, 1) in *Embodied Conflict: The Neural Basis of Conflict and Communication*. It's as though your nervous system is regularly asking itself, "Will the next moment be safe or dangerous?" This ability to scan your surroundings and anticipate events before they happen has been selected for evolutionarily.

Part of cultivating an open state of mind involves relaxing your inborn anticipatory tendency when you're actually safe but rumination still fuels your anxiety. The more you can become aware of the ways you regularly scan, anticipate, and expect danger when it's safe to relax, the more you can *be with* what's happening. Getting to know your vulnerabilities as lived experiences rather than feared thoughts is at the heart of opening.

Using Anchors to Relax

There's a twinge of pain in your lower back. You're dragging a heavy suitcase through an airport. Instead of getting lost in rumination about how it's your partner's fault for overpacking, you can be with the sensation for a few seconds. Then you can take some action that will help you resolve the problem. You might ask your partner for assistance, find an airport employee who can help you, or locate a trolley. The twinge of pain can remain a brief sensation rather than turning into a full-blown rumination cycle of blame or self-pity. If you sense anger or an impulse to kick the suitcase or yell at your partner, you might note these experiences with self-compassion. Has a threat link been activated? Do you have an attachment fear in this situation that would be worth exploring? You can use what you learn about yourself to inform how and what you communicate with your partner in the future concerning suitcases and packing for trips.

Awareness anchors support you in this practice of letting go of scanning and anticipating so you can open and be with inner experiences. They are used in many spiritual traditions, including Zen Buddhism and Vipassana meditation. They serve a range of purposes, from reducing mental chatter to achieving enlightenment. We'll use them to relax the body and calm the mind so you can open.

The breath, sensation, sounds, and awareness itself are four commonly used awareness anchors. As you experiment with the guided meditation that accompanies each anchor in the sections below, notice if there's one that fits you more than the others. Some people use different anchors in different situations, but others prefer to use one consistently.

Using awareness anchors can shift your focus from passive thoughts in the mind to sensory experiences in your body. This can bring sensations, emotions, and impulses into the foreground. Awareness anchors locate you squarely in the here and now, rather than in an upsetting memory of something you can't change or in thoughts about a dreaded future you can't know or control. When you're present and connected to your body, you're more likely to notice the vulnerability trio because you're not being distracted by overthinking.

Use any of the awareness anchors outlined below to practice opening. Follow the sequence of steps suggested for each anchor, or go to http://www.newharbinger.com/50034 and listen to the guided audios. Use these anchors when a specific trigger sets you off, when you're ruminating, or when you feel disconnected from yourself. The more regularly you practice anchoring, the more you'll be able to *be with* what's happening in the here and now. You'll begin cultivating the ability to open in response to specific triggers.

Leaning into a growth mindset, shifting from *thinking about* people and events to *being with* the way you experience them, and using awareness anchors to relax and open in the here and now are all practices that can help you foster a receptive state of mind.

Breath Anchoring

To anchor in the breath, bring awareness to the natural flow of your own breathing. Although it's important to breathe through your mouth when you need to, research has shown that nostril breathing is better for overall health (Nestor 2020).

Breathing usually has a consistent rhythm, though this rhythm changes and varies. With each breath, there are sensations you can track as you attend to the process of inhaling and exhaling, something you've already practiced in the "Getting Grounded in One Breath" exercise. Air flows against your upper lip. It cools your nostrils as you inhale and warms them as you exhale. Physical sensations, emotions, impulses, and thoughts can all arise in connection with the inhale-exhale cycle.

There are plenty of breathing techniques, styles, and methods you can experiment with if you find anchoring in breath settles and opens you. *Breath focus technique* links each breath with a word like "calm," "peace," or "relax." *Equal breathing* balances the inhale and the exhale by keeping them the same length—around three seconds long. *Holotropic Breathwork* guides practitioners through a two-part mouth-breathing cycle to relax and connect more deeply with themselves (Grof and Grof 2010).

SOLO EXERCISE: Breath Anchoring

Follow this sequence of steps to anchor in the breath. For a guided audio of breath anchoring, go to http://www.newharbinger.com/50034.

1. Find a place free of responsibilities and distractions where you can sit in a comfortable position while remaining alert. Sit with your body upright and your hands resting lightly on your knees or in your lap.

2. Bring awareness to your breathing, without changing anything about it. Simply allow your breath to flow naturally and effortlessly. Notice the air moving at your nostrils and upper lip, keeping your attention focused on one subtle experience at a time. Notice your ribs expanding and contracting with each inhale and each exhale.

3. When thoughts surface or a rumination cycle begins, gently let go of these thoughts without getting caught up in them and return to step 2, redirecting attention to your breathing. Continue tuning in to the subtle sensations at your nostrils and upper lip. Continue noticing the physical sensations of your ribs expanding and contracting with each inhale and each exhale.

Sensation Anchoring

Coming to our senses—literally—is the most immediate path to opening. In his book *Embodied Conflict: The Neural Basis of Conflict and Communication*, Tim Hicks (2018) writes, "Our interface with the external world is entirely and exclusively mediated by our five senses" (2). In our busy, everyday lives, the decibel level of our sensory experiences is turned up so high we're usually only aware of the flashiest, loudest, brightest inputs: strong colors; quick movements; the bass and treble of sounds in our immediate surroundings; salty, sweet, and savory tastes; strong smells that surprise, repel, or magnetize us; blatantly pleasurable or painful touches. These dramatic stimuli are some of what's available to us through our senses, but the vast majority of our sensations are subtle and hum along unremarked in the background.

Sitting quietly and closing your eyes can support you in opening to sensation. Try to notice one sensation at a time. You may feel a tingle along your skin or an itch at the back of your neck. You may notice prickles or pulses or become aware of the flow of energy in your arms. Or you may perceive a mix of these things.

To use sensation as an anchor, tune in to your body. Connect with the solidity or softness of the chair you're sitting on. Sense the coolness or warmth of air contacting your skin, the tickle of hair shifting slightly at your cheek or neck. Pick up on the pressure of waistbands and seams of clothing, or on the tightness in your shoulders or back. You may experience a dull ache or a cool spaciousness in your belly. All kinds of sensations surface in your body regularly.

Some sensations are strong, overt, and clear. Others are nearly imperceptible. Pay attention to what's arising. Don't judge sensations or try to get rid of the uncomfortable ones. Resist the temptation to make the pleasant ones last longer. Open up to what's happening right now and as you do, gently and attentively experience it.

SOLO EXERCISE: Sensation Anchoring

Follow this sequence of steps to anchor in sensations. For a guided audio of sensation anchoring, go to http://www.newharbinger.com/50034.

1. Find a comfortable place free of responsibilities and distractions. Sit in a relaxed position while remaining alert. Maintain your torso upright and your hands resting lightly on your knees or in your lap.

2. Bring awareness to your body in the here and now and notice any sensation that's here. Allow it to be exactly as it is without changing it, making it go away, or holding on to it. Stay with your experience of the sensations you're noticing from one moment to the next. Allow them to shift and change. When new sensations arise, let them become the focal point of your attention.

3. When thoughts surface or you catch a rumination cycle spinning, gently let go of these thoughts without getting caught up in them and return to step 2, redirecting attention to your body in the here and now. Tune in to any sensations arising in this moment, allowing them to float in awareness. Notice how sensations come and go, intensify, peak, and fade, and how new sensations arise.

Sound Anchoring

There are different ways to use sound as an anchor for awareness. You can listen to prerecorded, soothing sounds, such as quiet instrumental music. You can find a place where soothing sounds arise naturally, such as near a beach, on a porch, or in a laundromat. Or you can anchor in ambient noise present in your surroundings—such as a refrigerator buzzing, rain on a window, a radiator rattling, or the rumble of distant cars.

Sounds are vibrations traveling in waveforms through a medium (such as air). When they arrive at your eardrums, your brain translates them into perceptions. If you bring single-focused attention to any sound you hear, it can be used as an awareness anchor. You can notice individual sounds or the symphony created by their interplay.

Unpleasant or undesirable sounds can also serve as awareness anchors. A car alarm is composed of the same stuff as birdsong. The emotional reactions and meanings we link to sounds are events occurring within us. They aren't a part of the sound itself. If you're trying out sound anchoring for the first time, you may find neutral or pleasant sounds easier to anchor in than sharp, harsh, or unpleasant ones.

SOLO EXERCISE: Sound Anchoring

Follow this sequence of steps to anchor in sound. For a guided audio of sound anchoring, go to http://www.newharbinger.com/50034.

1. Find a place free of responsibilities and distractions where you can sit in a comfortable position. Remain alert. Sit with your torso upright and your hands resting lightly on your knees or in your lap.

2. Bring awareness to any sound in your environment. Lightly track what you hear with your focus on one sound at a time. Stay connected to what you're attending to from the moment a sound arises until it fades away.

3. When thoughts surface or a rumination cycle spins, gently let go of these thoughts without getting caught up in them and return to step 2, redirecting attention back to sound in your environment. Tune in to the nuances of what you're hearing, and to the vibrations, echoes, and silences between sounds as they begin and end.

Awareness Anchoring

A subtler and more elusive anchor than the ones we've explored so far is awareness itself.

In my twenties, I attended a lecture at the New York Insight Meditation Center in Manhattan where I was first introduced to the idea of anchoring in awareness. A mindfulness teacher spoke about the challenges and benefits of observing your mind, thoughts, and ultimately, awareness itself. When he invited those of us present to become aware of our own awareness, I was momentarily overcome by vertigo. Following the teacher's guidance left me feeling as if I was looking back at the light coming out of an old movie projector rather than attending to the images in front of me on the movie screen. It was like I'd turned myself inside out to get a look at my own eyeballs. When you saw your own eyeballs, I wondered, didn't it mean you had cataracts or floaters? Were we *meant* to be aware of our own awareness?

Since then, I've realized that this kind of anchoring isn't about turning yourself inside out or striving to do something unnatural. It's about consciously resting in the vibrant spaciousness within you and around you. Anchoring in awareness is something you probably already do without realizing it. Maybe you've felt it in peaceful or calm moments when you've connected to something bigger than your own personal identity.

Or maybe you've experienced it in the midst of highly emotional moments. Sometimes, in the middle of a fight with a partner about something all-important a moment earlier, we become aware of ourselves being aware of ourselves and suddenly the conflict strikes us as trivial and absurd. This awareness-aware-of-itself experience can happen at any time. I've heard people say they've had it while gazing at a baby's face, walking through the woods alone, listening to waves, and even doing something as ordinary as searching for lost change in a parking lot outside of a strip mall. It can happen anytime, anywhere.

With rumination cycles temporarily suspended, nothing interferes with a direct, open connection to the present. You're not thinking about this moment or your subjective experience of it. Awareness can become its own focus. The mental structures and patterns reinforcing a sense of separation between you and the world temporarily fade. For a second or two, you know yourself as boundless—as the space within you, around you, and between you and the world.

SOLO EXERCISE: Awareness Anchoring

Follow this sequence of steps to anchor in awareness itself. For a guided audio on anchoring in awareness, go to http://www.newharbinger.com/50034.

1. Find a place free of responsibilities and distractions where you can sit in a comfortable, relaxed position. Remain alert. Sit with your torso upright and your hands resting on your knees or in your lap.

2. Bring awareness to your own awareness. Sense it threaded through your body and extending out around you and beyond you. Rest in this experience as you let go of any mental effort to do anything. Let yourself float in this awareness-aware-of-itself experience.

3. When thoughts enter your mind or a rumination cycle spins, gently let go of these thoughts without getting caught up in them and return to step 2, redirecting attention to your own awareness and resting here.

Using Several Anchors at Once

You may find yourself shifting between several anchors in one sitting. Whenever you use awareness anchors as tools to relax and open, you'll naturally get distracted by your own thoughts. Then, you'll return to your anchor. Thoughts are not a problem in and of themselves. They're signs that you're aware because you're able to see them. Recognizing thoughts and returning to your awareness anchor repeatedly *is* the practice.

You may begin grounding yourself in the breath and then, after several breaths, get caught up in thinking about something you forgot to do or an email you've been meaning to write. When you notice you're thinking about any subject, return to single-tasking and refocus on your anchor. You might notice a constriction in your chest and focus on that, tracking the sensation for as long as you're able to before shifting to the next sensation that surfaces. Or you might return your focus to your breath.

When more thoughts arise—as they will—and you lose your anchor again, redirect attention to a new sensation, to your breath, to a sound (such as the distant siren of an ambulance or the shrill barking of a dog), or to awareness itself. The important thing to keep in mind about awareness anchors isn't sticking with one of them—though some people find that helpful. It's using them to reorient yourself from passive, reflexive thinking to the present, the only space where opening can ever happen.

JOINT EXERCISE: My Anchor

You can go through this exercise side by side in the same room with your partner or alone in different locations. Once you've tried using all four of the awareness anchors described in this chapter, write your answers to each of the questions below in a journal. Take turns sharing when you're done, referring to the Speaker and Listener responsibilities in the introduction for a refresher on creating safety and supporting connection.

* Which anchor felt most natural?

* Which anchor felt least natural?

* Did anything get in the way of exploring the anchors (impatience, rumination cycles, boredom, lack of curiosity, confusion, self-doubt, or attachment to a predetermined outcome)?

* What could you do to overcome this block?

* When might you benefit from using one (or more) of these anchors?

* What would support you in using this anchor more regularly?

Relationship rumination is a symptom of an allergy we've developed to our own vulnerability. To be intimate with ourselves and our partner, we need to increase our ability to open up to and experience what we reflexively block with overthinking. Opening in the third step of SLOW means assuming a relaxed, curious, receptive stance, including when you want to shut down. This takes practice. Awareness anchors can help by grounding you in the here and now so you can stay present, relaxed and open even when ruminative thoughts arise. In the fourth and final step of SLOW, you'll welcome previously rejected experiences and vulnerabilities into your self-concept, life, and relationship.

CHAPTER 7

Welcome Vulnerability and the Unknown to Be Who You Are

I didn't have a television, growing up. When I could get away with it, I used to visit one of the kids in my neighborhood after school and watch my favorite TV shows at her house. Her parents were kind and welcoming. Even if she was away at a piano lesson or horseback riding when I showed up, her mother always invited me in, asked about my day, and gave me a snack. Sometimes her father helped me with my math homework.

Their kindness started with the welcome mat on their porch, outside their front door. As I walked up the last steps of the long flight that led to their house, the mat always greeted me with the word "Welcome." Whenever I saw it, I felt special. The word was magic. It still is.

Genuinely welcoming someone—or something—into your orbit is a radical act. It extends the boundary of what you consider a part of the "me" you identify as yourself. Our partners do this with us when they accept us as we are. Maybe they've harped on something we do that they don't like, but today, they shrug and say, "I'll live with it because I love you." Welcoming is powerful. It changes irreconcilable differences into reconcilable ones.

Welcoming can also be powerful when applied to your own vulnerability. Welcome mats like the one on my neighbor's porch may not do anything for you, but those scraps of synthetic fiber still represent a meaningful stance as you complete your SLOW practice. By accepting what you've exiled or failed to include in your definition of "me," you grow. You embrace more of the complex, tender, mighty, vulnerable being you already are. By changing your stance, you change yourself. Welcoming supercharges a growth mindset.

Step four of SLOW is your psychological welcome mat. It's a call to connection, an affirmation of wholeness. It's a commitment to receiving all of yourself. Nothing about you has to be excluded from awareness or denied attention. You're not obligated to continue spinning rumination cycles or overthinking in your relationship as a defense against what's happening in the moment—and against your own vulnerability.

What's Under This?

How do you let your unconscious know you're ready to assume a welcoming stance?

One way is by asking a question: "What's under this?"

Although there's no actual physical "under" or "over" within our psyches, this question communicates: *I can take in what I've pushed out of my own awareness. I'm ready to recognize and accept what's here.*

In welcoming, you're communicating with a part of you that lies beyond your analytical mind. Having practiced opening, you're more relaxed and present. You've increased your comfort level with uncertainty. But this doesn't mean that what arises within you will come in an easy-to-grasp, pat answer. The response to this question will most likely be wordless and organic. Resist the urge to jump in with your problem-solving mind and *think* the answer. Hold off of on theorizing. Settle in and wait. Practice patience, curiosity, and nonattachment. Resist the temptation to hop around on your *thinking about* leg.

It's okay *not* to understand the way your body responds as you listen and wait. Maybe you'll notice wisps of emotion. Or you might sense a surge of energy. There may be a twinge of discomfort or a rise in physical tension. Whatever it is, be with it while remaining grounded in your body, open, and tuned in. Sometimes, sustained, focused attention alone can amplify what your body is communicating and bring clarity.

You'll always get an answer in some form. The absence of a response is also an answer. The answer you get doesn't have to make rational sense. The answer may come over the course of a minute, a day, or a week. It may come piecemeal, in seemingly random insights.

Whatever arises, welcome it.

Welcoming Vulnerability

In *Resilient: How to Grow an Unshakable Core of Calm, Strength, and Happiness,* Rick and Forrest Hanson (2018) talk about the importance of *activating* and *installing* positive states. When you do this regularly, lasting change roots in the neural structures of your brain. Activation takes place in SLOW when the threat link connects a trigger and your amygdala-based experience of danger while you remain present. You don't get lost in overthinking. A process that has happened mostly outside of your awareness starts to happen within it.

Activation is one part of this powerful change process. For a new, positive state or experience to stick, it also needs to be *installed.* In the Hansons' definition, installation is when experiences and states get locked into the brain's long-term storage. Although the neuroscience of this process is complex and still being understood and researched, it's clear that once they're stored, the positive states and experiences you've activated through healthy practices can become lasting traits and resources you're able to draw on more reliably.

Seeing and labeling your thoughts and rumination cycles and practicing SLOW pairs new, positive experiences with feared triggers. So does using personal and partner cues as warning lights. By accessing desirable states, like relaxation, curiosity, patience, and nonattachment, *while* experiencing a historically conditioned sense of threat (such as when you're triggered), the amygdala's code-red signal can shift to code yellow. The threat becomes less threatening. You reduce anxiety. You ruminate less.

Take Kerri, whom you met in chapter 1 and followed through her discovery of Margo's emotional affair in chapter 5. When something or someone triggers memories of the affair, Kerri practices shifting the amygdala's code-red signal to code yellow. She gets grounded in one breath or uses an awareness anchor to help her relax and connect with her experience in the here and now, including her vulnerabilities, emotions, sensations, impulses, and attachment fears. She pairs desirable states, like curiosity and calm, with feared triggers, like reminders of Margo's colleague.

Spending time with your own emotions and internal states—whether comfortable or uncomfortable—weakens your habitual relationship rumination by "converting the experiences [you are] already having into durable changes in neural structure and function" (Hanson and Hanson 2018, 57). When Michael, from chapter 4, practices seeing his negative thoughts, labeling his self-pity cycle and *being with* his own sensations and emotions in moments when Darlene asks him to be mindful about something—such as drinking when they go out—he's "installing" a new experience in his brain: relaxing into his vulnerabilities rather than tensing up, bracing himself against them, and blocking them with thoughts like, *She tries to control everything I do, nobody has any faith in me,* and *it's not fair.* This gives him the opportunity to experience what Darlene's words evoke in him in the form of sensations, emotions, and impulses and to connect with his attachment fears. Opening to what's happening in the moment becomes a new option for him.

Installation is when you psychologically metabolize something new. Because it's new, it may be hard for you to immediately digest or take in. When you install vulnerable experiences, you welcome them as fully *yours.* They're no longer locked away in a safety deposit box in the basement of your mind with an access code you can't remember. They're in an easy-to-access, color-coded file in your long-term brain storage, available when you need them.

The point at which vulnerable experiences transition from code-red to code yellow isn't clear-cut or absolute. Even after Michael has connected with the vulnerabilities evoked in him by Darlene's words—such as feelings of helplessness and fear of losing himself as he often did when he was a child growing up with his anxious, and sometimes intrusive, mother—it doesn't mean he won't ruminate again the next time Darlene says something he experiences as controlling. Just because Kerri has learned to see her thoughts and rumination cycles and feel some of her anger toward Margo rather than ruminating or getting depressed doesn't mean she won't doubt Margo's commitment to her. What it *does* mean is that both Michael and Kerri have expanded their self- and relationship-care options.

Even if old and new triggers still sometimes lead to rumination, Michael and Kerri are better equipped to *be with*, know, and welcome themselves as they are—with their triggers, warning lights, attachment fears, and vulnerabilities. The more you know and welcome yourself—through your sensations, impulses, and emotions—the easier it is to show up authentically in your relationship without relying on rumination to cope.

Welcome Sensations

Most of us have complicated relationships with our bodies. We may think we're at their mercy. We wonder why we were born into this particular body we don't like. We may resent our bodies for failing to give us what we want. We may wish we were stronger, healthier, fertile, energetic, agile, virile, feminine, or youthful.

Our bodies may have collapsed or submitted in situations when we wish they'd stood strong or fought back. They may have betrayed our emotional secrets, trembling, sweating, or flushing red with embarrassment when we wanted to maintain a calm façade. They may have shed tears when we wanted them to convey indifference. They may have stumbled on the way to the podium or stuttered into the mic against our will when we wanted to exude confidence.

To welcome what you notice through your five senses, begin by appreciating your body as it is. Stand in front of a mirror and imagine seeing yourself through the eyes of a being who loves you just as you are, in exactly the body you're in. Tell each part of your body, "I welcome you." Pay attention to sensations in the body part you're welcoming—or anywhere else you feel them.

Your body doesn't communicate with words the way you do. It speaks in tingles, aches, constriction, spaciousness, queasiness, and surges of warmth and heat, coolness, or iciness. It releases tension through yawns and sighs. It communicates through pleasure, pain, hunger, nausea, vertigo, and discomfort. Recognize any bias you hold favoring "rational" thinking. By welcoming sensations, you prioritize the unique syntax and grammar of your body's messages.

SOLO EXERCISE: Welcoming My Sensations

Find a quiet, private space, such as a bathroom, where you won't be disturbed. Stand in front of a mirror if possible. You can set the tone by playing calming music or lighting a candle. The more of your body you can see, the more of it you can practice welcoming. Don't be afraid to get completely naked for this exercise.

Allow your eyes to rest on the body part you're welcoming (if it's visible) as you say each phrase below. If it's not visible, imagine it. Pay attention to (or imagine) its color, texture, and shape. How has this part supported you? Bring awareness to the ways it has been there for you your entire life. Read the statements below, pausing after each one to notice any sensations that arise.

Welcome, face.

Welcome, ears.

Welcome, lips.

Welcome, eyes.

Welcome, head.

Welcome, brain.

Welcome, neck.

Welcome, shoulders.

Welcome, arms.

Welcome, hands.

Welcome, chest/breasts.

Welcome, heart.

Welcome, lungs.

Welcome, stomach.

Welcome, intestines.

Welcome, blood.

Welcome, vulva/clitoris/penis.

Welcome, womb/ovaries/testicles.

Welcome, anus.

Welcome, thighs.

Welcome, knees.

Welcome, calves.

Welcome, bones.

Welcome, feet.

Welcome Impulses

Urges and impulses can guide you toward creation, change, expression, connection, and self-preservation. If you feel a prickle of heat at the mention of your uncle's name and an urge to clean the attic, try *being with* this urge or impulse rather than acting it out or suppressing it. *Being with* an impulse can help you know what you want—even if you don't act on it. If you block impulses, you inhibit your own inner wisdom, power, creativity, and action potential.

Knowing your impulses can help you value your needs, desires, and wants. Impulses can guide you to remember buried longings. They can nudge you toward self-preservation and self-advocacy when necessary and toward taking up more psychic, emotional, and physical space rather than habitually accommodating others to your own detriment. They can encourage you to share your opinion in a conversation where you normally stay silent. Impulses can propel you toward self-expression, pursuing your dreams, and setting healthy boundaries.

Being aware of your urges and impulses won't automatically cause you to follow them—quite the opposite. When you're able to be more aware of your own impulses, you become *less* impulsive. It's when you *don't* attend to or welcome your impulses that they blindside you. Rejected impulses rarely bow out gracefully and vanish into thin air. They fester, leading to passive-aggression and thoughtless actions you later regret. Welcoming impulses means *being with* your impulses and experiencing them as a part of who you are, even when you don't believe acting on them is the right choice for you.

Impulses show up as recurring sensations drawing you toward movement or motion. They're not the destination. They're like street signs that say "This Way," pointing you in a general direction. It's up to you to figure out the specific route. You can practice welcoming impulses by noticing an impulse and expressing it as fully as possible, as long as it's safe to do so. For example, if you're in your office and you have an impulse to slump down in your chair, follow the impulse and see what happens. Experience what it's like to slump. You might even exaggerate this impulse if you have privacy and slump all the way down to the floor. Allow gravity to pull on you as though you weighed a thousand pounds.

If your foot is shaking, shake your whole leg—or even your body. Sometimes after threatening or scary situations, our body needs to discharge nervous energy the way gazelles do when they narrowly escape predators (Levine 1997). Notice what it feels like to shake. If you have the impulse to cross your arms over your chest, do it fully and consciously. Give yourself a bear hug. Or pout like a child. Feel the impulse and what's behind it fully.

If you have a history of being impulsive, you'll take a different approach. If you're someone who struggles with acting mindlessly on your impulses without pausing to consider whether what you're doing is what you truly want to do, notice and contain your impulses. Practice simply *being with* them as you remain aware of them, but without taking any visible action. Connect with the experience of impulses arising and moving through your body as energy or in the form of sensations.

In order to welcome impulses, it's important to practice experiencing them safely, with awareness and curiosity. Welcome them as they are. Get to know them. Consider whether it's in your best interest to move in the direction of their "This Way" signs.

SOLO EXERCISE: Welcoming My Impulses

In a journal, at the top of a page, write "Sensation," "Impulse," "I Welcomed It By," and "How That Felt." Throughout the day, notice any recurring sensations in your body and see if there are any impulses connected to them. Then, practice welcoming impulses by finding a movement, gesture, or action that expresses them safely and more fully than you normally would. If you have a history of being impulsive or mindlessly acting out your impulses without considering whether or not they're aligned with what you truly want, practice containing them, being with them, and experiencing them internally *without* expressing them.

For example, you might write, "heavy head, tired arms" under "Sensation," "curl up in a ball" under "Impulse," "I curled up on the floor of my office in a ball for one minute" under "I Welcomed It By," and "silly, sad, freeing" under "How That Felt." For a PDF worksheet of this exercise, go to http://www.new harbinger.com/50034.

Welcome Emotions

Emotions ebb and flow within you and between you and your partner (and others). No matter how logical, reasonable, practical, thoughtful, intellectual, or action-oriented you are, you're also emotional. If you're stoic about everything, don't cry, and appear calm and neutral at all times, emotions still rise and recede within you. They're like tides. Sometimes they move under a still, mirrorlike surface. You can have them in the way a frozen bay can still have water. Whether or not you notice the flow of emotional currents within you, they shape choices you make. To welcome emotions, you first have to accept a basic fact: you *have* emotions. You have a lot of them. Often.

It's not unusual for people who regularly avoid their emotions to find themselves attracted to partners who are very emotionally expressive. If you view intellect as superior to emotions, your triggers with your partner will center around their oversensitivity, emotional outbursts, unpredictability, possessiveness, irrationality, controlling behaviors, and neediness. Their triggers with you will relate to your emotional inhibition, complacency, coldness, insensitivity, and overreliance on reason and logic.

When you ask, "What's under this?" tune in to any emotions you're aware of in the moment. Bring attention to emotional undercurrents within you. Turning your attention to your emotions is like adjusting the dial on a vintage radio. There's no single place in your body where you'll find or feel emotions all the time (though it's common to feel them in the torso, the area of the body between the throat and the pelvic floor). Give yourself permission to feel. Be curious. Which emotions seem to be shifting, flowing, or blocked?

Resist any tendency to analyze what arises. Stay connected to your body—especially to your torso. Wait for a response to surface in your body's language. Remember the six basic emotions: happiness, sadness, fear, disgust, anger, and surprise. Notice if any of these are present.

SOLO EXERCISE: Welcoming My Emotions

Take a moment to close your eyes. Use the "Getting Grounded in One Breath" exercise or one of the awareness anchors we explored in the last chapter to help you relax.

Ask yourself, "What's under these anxious thoughts, this trigger, or this upsetting situation?"

Remember the six basic emotions: happiness, sadness, fear, disgust, anger, and surprise. Notice if any of these are present. If none of these resonate with you, check in for other emotions or feelings. Many people can identify with feeling helpless, restless, vulnerable, or lonely in challenging situations. Depending on what you're feeling, practice saying:

"I welcome this happiness."

"I welcome this sadness."

"I welcome this fear."

"I welcome this disgust."

"I welcome this anger."

"I welcome this surprise."

"I welcome this helplessness."

"I welcome this vulnerability."

"I welcome this loneliness."

"I welcome this restlessness."

SOLO EXERCISE: Welcoming What's Here

When you feel upset, uncomfortable, or unsettled, take a moment to identify what you're aware of in your body. Start by choosing something minor, such as your partner leaving their dirty dishes on the counter or repeating a question you answered a couple of minutes after you answered it. Once you get comfortable with this process, you can practice with more challenging, higher-intensity triggers.

Use an awareness anchor to relax and label what you notice along with the location of sensations, impulses, or emotional experiences (for example, "I feel tension in my shoulders," "I feel sadness behind my eyes," "I feel tightness in my jaw," "I feel queasiness in my stomach," "I feel nervous energy in my arms"). Rest one of your hands on the place where the sensations, emotions, or impulses are strongest (for example, the chest, abdomen, or jaw). Visualize what you're sensing or noticing as something you could hold with tenderness and affection: a child, a small forest creature, or a colored ball of energy.

Transmit your approval and acceptance to this vulnerable experience through the hand resting against your body. You might say, "It's okay. I'm here. I welcome this sensation, impulse, or emotion." Notice any subtle shifts or changes that take place in your body as you welcome.

JOINT EXERCISE: Welcoming Review

In a journal, write your answers to the questions below. Refer to the Speaker and Listener responsibilities in the introduction for a refresher on creating safety and supporting connection as you share your answers.

* What do you imagine will be your biggest challenge with welcoming?

* What tool or strategy from earlier chapters might help you overcome this challenge?

* How do you think welcoming can empower you?

Welcoming someone—or something—into your orbit is a radical act. It extends the boundary of what you consider a part of the "me" you identify as yourself. Once you see, label, and open, the question "What's under this?" extends an invitation to your unconscious, letting it know you're available, curious, and attentive. Welcoming your vulnerabilities means assuming a receptive stance and tuning in to sensations, emotions, and impulses. But remember: Your unconscious doesn't communicate with words the way your conscious mind does. It communicates in wisps of emotion, tingles, aches, sensations, surges of heat or iciness, tension, and spaciousness. Now that you've learned the four steps of SLOW, you can begin practicing SLOW in the trenches of your relationship. In the next chapter, we'll look at some tips that can help.

CHAPTER 8

Tips for Applying the SLOW Process

Two people can use SLOW for the same rumination cycle, the same trigger, and within the same relationship, and each of their trajectories will be unique. Not only will each person's process unfold differently, it will unfold differently each time for the same person. This is because SLOW is a big-picture view of a wild, thriving inner landscape far more than a set of Google map directions for navigating something predictable and fixed. SLOW won't show you a linear route. But it will provide signposts to keep you on track as you nurture and foster qualities in yourself that support a growth mindset. It will also help you practice *being with* what's happening when you catch rumination pinwheels spinning.

Here are four basic ways you can use SLOW:

1.   After the fact

2.   On the spot

3.   Alone

4.   With a partner

How and when you use SLOW will depend on how much time you have, where you are, your motivation level, and your ease guiding and being guided.

SLOW After the Fact

Steven and Masie are sitting by a pool in Miami. Masie has commented on the sunset. She mentions returning to this same resort next year. Steven immediately gets anxious. *She can't enjoy the moment,* he thinks. *She's already planning next year's vacation. If we come here regularly, we'll go broke. It's going to take me six months as it is to pay off my credit card bill for this trip.*

"Are you okay?" she asks. "Did I say something wrong?"

Steven rolls his eyes and exhales.

"Why can't you just enjoy being here *now?*" he asks.

The hostility in his voice confirms Masie's fear: something *is* wrong.

She stays quiet as her own ruminative thoughts start spinning. *He's so touchy. I thought going away would help us, but here we are, disconnected again. I should have kept my mouth shut. He always overreacts.*

Later, while Masie naps, Steven sits on the balcony of their hotel room and reflects. Using SLOW after the fact, he sees he was ruminating by the pool and labels the trigger: Masie's comment about returning next year. Steven anchors in sensation, feeling his bare feet against the cool terrace. As he relaxes, he transitions into opening, and asks, "What's under this?"

Pressure builds behind his eyes. His chest tightens. He feels sad. His mother and father argued a lot about money when he was a kid. They worried about the future. Steven senses a connection between these memories of his parents and his frustration with Masie whenever she talks about the future, especially if what she's saying involves spending money.

"I welcome this sadness," Steven says to himself as the surf recedes on the beach below. He has gained some clarity about what set off his rumination cycle with Masie by the pool, and he senses that his frustration has diminished. It occurs to him that her comment was probably her way of letting him know how much she was enjoying being on vacation with him.

It can be easier to see your overthinking calmly and objectively in retrospect, when you're not caught up in the situation triggering it. Using

SLOW after the fact can heighten your awareness of triggers, vulnerabilities, and attachment fears, increasing the likelihood that you'll notice them in the future when they crop up again rather than reacting to them defensively.

SLOW On the Spot

When you use SLOW on the spot, you're catching your rumination in the moment and moving through the four steps in a seamless flow to shift your automatic threat reaction and reorient yourself to reality on the fly. This can help you pivot out of a fear-based response.

Let's revisit the above example with Steven and Masie. They're sitting by the pool at the Miami resort, and Masie has just commented on the sunset, mentioning how much she'd like to return next year. This time, using SLOW on the spot, Steven recognizes the heightened anxiety he feels in the wake of Masie's comment as one of his warning lights. Remembering SLOW, he takes a moment to see his thoughts *as* thoughts. He labels them by making a mental note of the ones he's aware of: *She can't enjoy the moment. She's already planning next year's vacation. We'll go broke.* He taps into the punishing, anxious tone of these thoughts, seeing them as the beginnings of a hybrid blame and worry cycle. His threat link has gotten activated. He reminds himself that these thoughts are simply thoughts—pseudofacts in the form of assumptions and predictions. He has moved through the first two steps of SLOW on the spot.

"Are you okay?" Masie asks. "Did I say something wrong?"

He takes her hand and squeezes it.

"I was thinking about what you said," he responds.

In this situation, Steven might segue into step three of SLOW with the question, "I wonder what was under this anxious reaction?" even if he does this in his own mind as he gazes at the sunset with Masie lying next to him. If he's able to open and connect with his vulnerabilities or attachment fear, he could even share these with Masie. Or he might choose to enjoy the sunset without moving into this step. Since the amygdala's code-red signal has shifted to a code yellow through seeing and labeling, the experience of "threat" has lessened. Catching his worry and blame cycles before they got the better of him helped Steven interrupt a rumination cycle and stay present.

Getting a handle on your ruminative thinking as it's happening is a game changer. Even just a small, quick insight—such as seeing that a sequence of ruminative thoughts are thoughts or that these thoughts are the building blocks of a particular cycle—can help you change the lines you would normally recite in a dead-end script. Seeing and labeling blame, control, worry, doubt, and self-pity cycles makes it easier to disengage from a fear-based interpretation of reality to change the entire tenor of an interaction.

SLOW Alone

Guiding yourself through seeing, labeling, opening, and welcoming is at the foundation of a SLOW practice. The steps represented by the first letter of each word act as guardrails, making it easier for you to keep track of where you are in the process and to move through it in your own way and at your own pace. If you get off track, the steps represented by the first letter of each word remind you of where you are, where you left off, and where you can go next.

The more you practice guiding yourself through SLOW, the more familiar and organic the process becomes. Let yourself experiment. Notice what works for you. Some of the steps will likely overlap, blend together, or happen out of sequence at times. The steps can unfold and interweave as long as you practice *being with* and welcoming what arises.

SLOW with a Partner

Using SLOW together can help partners reduce rumination in their relationship field collaboratively as they also practice supporting one another's process in the guiding role. Before you try using SLOW with a partner, go through the steps on your own until you feel comfortable with them. Get familiar with the process. The more firsthand experience you have seeing, labeling, opening, and welcoming, the easier it will be to guide your partner.

Just as you've been sharing Speaker and Listener roles throughout this book, you can share roles with your partner when you guide one another through SLOW. The guiding partner will stay grounded and present as they offer prompts, similar to the way they do in the Listener role. The receiving partner will take the time they need with each prompt, staying connected to themselves and taking cues from their own sensations, emotions, and impulses as they open to what's happening in the moment. If you choose, you can share what you discover with your partner as you go, at the end of your process. You can also keep what you discover private.

JOINT EXERCISE: Partner-Guided SLOW

Sit comfortably across from each other. Decide who will be the guiding partner and who will be the receiving partner. The receiving partner can share their process out loud with the guiding partner following each prompt, or they can keep their discoveries to themselves for a more self-reflective practice. Agree on a signal you can use that lets the guiding partner know when you're ready to receive the next prompt (such as nodding your head or saying, "Ready").

Step	Guiding Partner Prompts	Receiving Partner Instructions
See	"Take a moment to 'see' your rumination cycle."	*Direct your attention inward and "see" your thoughts. Notice if you have been, or are, ruminating.*
Label	"Label your thoughts or your rumination cycle."	*Take a moment to put a few of your current thoughts into words. Can you sense an emotional undertone? Which cycle or cycles might they reflect?*

Open	"Notice what's under these thoughts or this cycle. Focus on your breath, sensations, sounds, or awareness as you relax and open."	*Be with what arises in the form of sensations, impulses, or emotions. Take your time. Stay grounded in your body.*
Welcome	"Can you welcome whatever arises?"	*Let yourself experience and welcome whatever arises with patience, curiosity, and nonattachment.*

JOINT EXERCISE: Reflections on Partner-Guided SLOW

In a journal, write your answer to the questions below. When you're done, share your answers, referring to the Speaker and Listener responsibilities described in the introduction.

* Which step or steps came naturally?

* Which step or steps did you struggle with?

* What was it like being guided through this process?

Four ways you can use SLOW are: after the fact, on the spot, alone, and with a partner.

The more you guide yourself through SLOW, the easier it will be to flow with the process. Using SLOW together can help partners reduce rumination in their relationship field collaboratively as they support one another in the guiding role. Finally, let's take a look at a few healthy thinking styles and useful skills that can go a long way toward nourishing love as you make SLOW a regular practice.

CHAPTER 9

Caring for Your Relationship

In medicine, there are different ways of approaching symptoms, pain, and disease. With preventive care, you take the long view, supporting strength, flexibility, health, and resilience in the future by taking good care of yourself today. By making sure your body, heart, and mind receive proper nourishment, you can prevent many illnesses from taking root. Palliative care focuses on reducing the severity of symptoms once they appear. This kind of care helps patients manage or accept ongoing symptoms by maintaining a high quality of life in the face of chronic or complex medical problems. Curative care treats and cures the disease or problem.

To avoid getting a cold, you get enough sleep, eat nutritious foods, exercise, reduce your stress level, and wear a face mask in crowded places. If you catch a cold, you change your approach and shift to palliative care. You increase your immunity by resting, avoiding stressful situations, taking vitamin C, and drinking lots of fluids to speed up your body's recovery. With many illnesses, palliative care segues into curative care. The more you can support your body's natural repair processes, the more quickly you'll heal on your own.

In relationships, these three types of care are interwoven. Preventive care reduces the need for palliative and curative care, and palliative care can become curative care over time.

Preventive Care: Healthy Thinking

You have an argument with your spouse. You didn't defend him at a party when a friend joked about his potbelly. In fact, you joined in with everyone else's laughter.

He shouldn't take himself so seriously, you think, when your spouse shares how your reaction hurt him. *It's not my fault he's touchy. He's way too sensitive. He shouldn't care so much about his appearance. If he doesn't want to be teased, he should exercise. Maybe I'll find him an article on the importance of having a sense of humor about your flaws.*

In this example, you may convince yourself you're engaging in the healthy thinking skills of self-reflection and problem solving. You've considered what happened and come up with a solution. If you sense the tone and function of these thoughts, however, you'll notice your reflections and solutions have a judgmental, defensive quality. You've identified the problem as your spouse's sensitivity rather than what his sensitivity evokes *in you.* If you practice SLOW, you may see your blame and control cycles, label them, and open to your own feelings of insecurity and shame about what you did. You may connect with memories from when you were the butt of people's jokes, or with your own vulnerable experiences related to belonging. You may even welcome these blocked experiences and feel more compassion toward your spouse.

When couples' thinking reflects what's happening in the world outside of them accurately, they're able to cope better as a team. Change isn't as scary when you and your partner can depend on each other to be honest and kind. Blame, worry, doubt, control, and self-pity cycles confuse and complicate change by layering new problems on top of the original hurt. They leak toxins into the relationship field, as we discussed in chapter 2. Healthy thinking helps couples resolve problems by working through conflicts—not avoiding them. When you know yourself, you can be clear with your partner about your boundaries and needs. Clarity reduces confusion.

If the mind made its own junk food, it would be overthinking. Overthinking fills a craving in the short term and harms your health over the long haul. As you wean yourself from it, you're practicing preventive care in your relationship. You're checking the ingredients on the side of the package for high-fructose corn syrup and sodium nitrate. Adaptive self-reflection, metacognition, emotional intelligence, problem solving, and positive reappraisal are five powerful and healthy thinking alternatives to rumination. Consider these healthy thinking options the mind's organic, farm-to-table produce.

Adaptive Self-Reflection

In *Women Who Think Too Much*, author and researcher Susan Nolen-Hoeksema (2003) suggests that the opposite of rumination is adaptive self-reflection. Adaptive self-reflection is when you focus on concrete aspects of a situation rather than on a situation in the abstract. If you're upset with your partner for complaining about the weather, for example, and you start ruminating about what a negative person they are and how you wish they knew how to appreciate life, you might shift gears using SLOW and decide to engage in adaptive self-reflection instead.

For example, if your partner says, "Ugh, I wanted to go for a walk, but it's cold and rainy today," and you start ruminating about their comment with thoughts like, *They always complain about everything. I'm miserable because they're so negative. Why can't they just be grateful?* you might see these thoughts and resist the urge to spin their complaint into a painful blame cycle of your own. You can recognize that your partner made one comment about the weather. They don't *always* complain about *everything*. You can remind yourself that it *is* cold and rainy today. You can remember that your partner is human and has negative feelings and low moods. You can distinguish between facts and pseudofacts.

In addition, you can place your attention on what you *can* control or change about your circumstances. Rather than wasting time and energy thinking about your partner's negativity, you might focus on something the two of you could do that would be fun, like make popcorn, cuddle on the couch, and watch a movie. Then, you can ask them if they want to do this with you or if they have another idea that might lift your spirits. You can't control the weather or your partner's feelings, but you can influence how you respond to the weather and to your partner. Adaptive self-reflection echoes the AA Serenity Prayer drawn from American theologian Reinhold Niebuhr's writings: *"God, grant me the serenity to accept the things I cannot change, courage to change the things I can, and the wisdom to know the difference"* (Shapiro 2014).

Metacognition

When you think about your thinking in a way that supports you and your relationships, you're using this skill. Metacognitive abilities are strengthened as you direct attention inward at key moments to "see" thoughts and thought patterns or to recognize cognitive strengths and limitations when accomplishing different tasks.

Remaining relaxed while your newly licensed partner drives your beloved car may require you to look out the window and think about something other than whether they're noticing stop signs or turning off their blinker. Metacognition helps you know this. If you spin worry cycles about forgotten passports, missed planes, and other things going dreadfully wrong before a trip, metacognition skills make it possible for you to see this pattern and prepare for the trips you take in advance so that you can create happier, calmer travel conditions. Drawing on metacognitive skills is an essential part of preventive relationship care.

Emotional Intelligence

Emotional intelligence spans a range of healthy thinking skills. It includes experiencing emotions with awareness, expressing them, and considering your own and others' emotions during social interactions. This skill allows you to know and connect with yourself and others on a meaningful level. Although it can be categorized as a healthy thinking skill, emotional intelligence is threaded through many other skills that support relationships. Some of these include assertiveness, self-awareness, and self-regulation skills.

As Lisette notices that her own feelings of self-judgment and inadequacy have been fueling her reaction toward Manuel when he invites her closer to him in bed (from the story in chapter 1), she's practicing emotional intelligence. Her awareness of her own thoughts, feelings, and current relationship with her mother bridges her privately experienced vulnerabilities and how she makes sense of and communicates them to Manuel.

When you're able to be with and respect the healthy impulses embedded in your emotions, you can stay true to your needs rather than to someone else's expectations of you. Cultivating emotional intelligence helps you know and trust that there are healthy action tendencies latent in your emotions. When you're afraid, for example, you may have the impulse to flee from danger and toward protection. When you're angry, you may have an urge to fight, assert, defend, or set limits. When you're sad, you may sense a pull to seek support or grieve (Shapiro 2021). Developing emotional intelligence increases your capacity to experience, know, and contain a range of emotions. It also deepens your ability to empathize with your partner and communicate with them authentically.

As you strengthen your emotional intelligence skills, be aware of the difference between expressing an emotion and creating an emotional narrative. Emotional narratives are thoughts disguised as emotions. "I feel like breaking something." "I feel I did all I could." "I feel that you're avoiding me." These are descriptions, assessments, and mini stories—not emotions.

When you're looking to cultivate emotional intelligence, catch yourself when you express thoughts disguised as emotions, and then return to Eckman's basic six. Use single-emotion words to capture or connect with your *true* emotions, for example, "I feel angry," rather than "I feel like breaking something," "I feel helpless," rather than "I feel I did all I could," and "I feel sad," rather than "I feel that you don't care about me."

Saying the words that accurately match what you feel is one important facet of emotional intelligence. Attuning to yourself and your body is another essential part of this skill. The emotion words you use to describe your inner experiences will resonate if they're accurate and true for you.

Problem Solving

When you rely on your problem-solving abilities, you use abstract thought to review past experiences that can help you consider the current problem you're trying to solve from different angles. You also draw on your imagination to create an array of possible future scenarios. You assess the likelihood of future events, weigh options, factor in risks, and adapt your approach.

Picture your partner driving down a country road in the rain when the wheels of your car get stuck in the mud. You argue with them, asking why they weren't more careful. In an attempt to solve the problem, they rev the engine and sink the wheels deeper into the mud.

Problem solving involves pausing. Instead of mindlessly criticizing your partner or revving the engine to no avail, you take stock. You evaluate the problem together: your tires are stuck in the mud. Pumping the gas pedal won't help. You identify possible solutions as a team, such as placing floor mats from the car under the front tires or calling roadside assistance. When you're ready, you work together to test out your solutions.

Most relationship challenges won't be as concrete as this one. I use the wheels-in-the-mud example because it's a vivid metaphor. When it comes to the healthy thinking skill of problem solving, you will need to take your foot off the gas pedal of overthinking and redirect your energy from unproductive conflict to identifying solutions together. Do this by sharing ideas without judging one another. You will need to agree on which solutions to test out. Then, you can evaluate what you've done and see which solutions are most effective.

Positive Reappraisal

In *Burnout*, Nagoski and Nagoski (2019) describe positive reappraisal as deciding that the thing you're working toward is worth it—even if you're not reaching your goal yet. When you positively reappraise something, you reject whatever negative meaning your mind assigns to your current position relative to gaining, getting, or achieving your goal.

You distinguish the means from the end and recall your true priorities. You recommit and remain realistic.

If you're preparing a special breakfast in bed for your partner to celebrate your anniversary and you burn the last two pieces of toast, you may start spinning thoughts like, *Look what I've done. What's wrong with me? This isn't working! Here I am trying to do something nice, and I messed up. I'm incompetent.* In this example, your first reaction to the burned toast results in blame and self-pity cycles. You'd envisioned a perfect breakfast that will delight your partner. That vision has been sullied, and you blame yourself.

But maybe you can see your rumination cycle, label it, and remember that a picture-perfect breakfast isn't the point. It's just a means to an end—not an end in itself. You can refocus on your priority: celebrating your anniversary and expressing your love. Now you can continue making breakfast, however imperfect it turns out to be. Positively reappraised, the burned toast doesn't matter. It's a sign of your good intentions and determination—not of failure.

SOLO EXERCISE: Healthy Thinking

In a journal, write "Trigger" and "Rumination Cycle" at the top of a page. Identify one moment or incident that upset you and felt threatening and list it under "Trigger." Identify a few thoughts along with the rumination cycle that followed this moment or incident and write it under "Rumination Cycle." If you can't remember, make an educated guess. What thoughts typically follow this kind of trigger? What cycle do they reflect?

Make a list of the five different healthy thinking strategies we've identified in this chapter: adaptive self-reflection, metacognition, emotional intelligence, problem solving, and positive reappraisal. After each strategy, fill in a healthier thought response to the trigger you've identified that reflects this particular form of healthy thinking. For a PDF worksheet of this exercise, go to http://www.newharbinger.com/50034.

Palliative Care

First aid kits are collections of palliative care essentials. People keep them in trunks, purses, backpacks, and medicine cabinets so they can pull them out whenever they need sterile gauze, a Band-Aid, or disinfectant. When it comes to responding quickly to mishaps and accidents, it's important to have first aid kits handy. You never know when you'll need them.

But what about first aid kits for relationships? Isn't it just as important to have tried-and-true preventive, palliative, and curative care strategies and tools you can rely on for emotional mishaps, injuries, and misunderstandings? We need first aid kits that help us soothe our emotional cuts and scrapes and prevent relational injuries from getting worse.

Some basic but important palliative care tools you can use in your relationship every day to avoid relational injuries and to heal them when they happen are conscious communication, adult time-outs, the "yes, and" approach, adaptability, and kindness.

Conscious Communication

All forms of couples therapy teach some version of conscious communication. Cognitive-behavioral couple therapy (CBCT)—and before that behavioral couple therapy (BCT)—used the Speaker-Listener format, along with the problem-solving technique, to structure conscious and intentional communication (Baucom et al. 2015) between partners. It's used in the Prevention and Relationship Enhancement Program (PREP; Markman et al. 2010) and in integrative therapies, such as the Therapeutic Palette approach (Fraenkel 2009). It's also a part of integrative behavioral couple therapy (Christensen et al. 2015), Relational Life Therapy (Real 2007), the Gottman Method couples therapy (Gottman and Silver 2015), the Imago Dialogue in Imago Relationship Therapy (Hendrix and Hunt 1992), and emotionally focused therapy (EFT; Johnson 2008).

Learning to communicate intentionally and consciously with your partner is an ongoing practice. It's a combination of *intra*personal skills—how you relate to yourself—and *inter*personal skills—how you relate to others. Another way of saying this is: balancing self-care with relationship care supports conscious communication. When you practice intentional communication—as you've been doing in the Speaker and Listener roles—you attune to what's happening within you as well as within your relationship field. Eventually, you can rely on your conscious communication skills to support you even during intense, emotionally charged interactions when your threat link has been activated.

Adult Time-Outs

You're chatting with your partner, and suddenly, something they say rubs you the wrong way. You question them: How could they say something like that to you?

"You misinterpreted me," they respond. Or maybe they criticize you. "You're on edge today." How dare they suggest *you* are the problem! You get defensive.

Both of you talk, but you're not communicating. Your mouths move and words emerge, but there is no Listener listening to either of you. If there's no Listener, there's also no Speaker, even when both of you are talking. Your speech is pressured, the pitch of your voice has gotten higher. You're interrupting your partner, and they're interrupting your interruptions. Your conversation has gone way off the rails. Yet you still think you can convince your partner that they should apologize because they're wrong. You're at a crossroads. You have a choice.

What do you do? You can double down, speak faster than you already are, interrupt more, and continue raising the pitch of your voice—approaching near glass-shattering levels of shrillness. If your partner makes the same choice and ups the ante too, then you'll be in a full-on, no-holds-barred argument. Accusations unrelated to the original sticking point in your discussion will be flung back and forth, wrecking your plans for a pleasant evening. Negative emotions will spill out into the relationship field, along with half a dozen kitchen sinks. You may have already done this kind of thing in the past. The outcome isn't a mystery. It doesn't end well. At best, there will be a lot of emotional cleanup to do afterward.

You have another choice, though: you can take an adult time-out.

Most people think time-outs are for kids, not adults. But adult time-outs are for our *inner* adult kids. When you lose control of your ability to be either a Listener or a Speaker with your partner, you've turned into a peculiar combo: an adult-kid. We can all lose control of our ability to be Listeners and Speakers as we have adult tantrums. A trigger activates our threat link, cortisol floods our bodies, and we believe we're under attack. What we say or do in this state of mind won't improve things. We're trying to get rid of our discomfort rather than being with it.

When a fight escalates, the best thing you can do is remove yourself from the discussion, even if only for the time being. Create some space between you to protect you both from the kind of knee-jerk reactivity it's easier to engage in when you're in each other's field of vision. Give your nervous system at least ten minutes to settle. Here are three steps you can follow for an adult time-out:

1. Tell your partner you're going to take a break from your discussion, for how long, and why. For example: "I'm going upstairs for ten minutes to calm myself down so I can listen and talk to you about this subject calmly again."

2. Find a private place where you can sit down and use an awareness anchor.

3. Go through SLOW, seeing your thoughts, labeling the trigger that set you off, the attachment fears, and your rumination cycle. Open to what's under these things, including your own vulnerable experiences, and welcome what you discover.

The "Yes, And" Approach

You're in an improvisational theater troupe. A fellow actor says, "I'm in a brand-new $200,000 Tesla on my way to San Francisco listening to Billie Holiday and eating Doritos." Now, it's your turn to speak and offer a spontaneous line. You could dismiss their claim with, "No, your girl-friend just broke up with you over text, and you're crying in the backseat of an Uber." The foundation of improvisational theater isn't negation, though. It's affirmation.

You might, for example, say, "*Yes, and*...I'm riding a supersonic hov-erboard right next to you, flashing you the peace sign." As the improvi-sational piece you're creating unfolds in surprising and unpredictable ways, both actors have the opportunity to be present and engaged. Humor and spontaneity can emerge. Neither of them know what's going to happen next. What they do know is that whatever they offer will be received with *yes, and.* This understanding supports safety, trust, and flow.

As part of palliative relationship care, assume the *yes, and* attitude of improvisational theater actors. Always try to make room for your part-ner's perspective. When there are conflicts and you don't agree with your partner—or when their perspective is different from yours—practice a *yes, and* attitude. Differences are okay, even when they're hard to accept. But you can still listen without contradicting them. Your partner's feel-ings, views, and opinions matter. I'm not saying you have to *agree* with their feelings, views, and opinions. Being receptive isn't the same thing as agreement. Assuming a *yes, and* approach is a precursor to accepting your partner as they are. Because you both are *already* who you are, rejecting each other is an exercise in futility.

When Manuel and Lisette, from chapter 1, decide to renovate their bathroom, Manuel is excited. He feels like this is an opportunity to dem-onstrate his commitment to Lisette by investing in their home, putting time and research into selecting different types of tiles, finding the right vanity with a Carrara marble sink, and locating the perfect ceiling lamp. When the bathroom is done, it looks bright and inviting. Manuel is proud of what he has accomplished, and excited about the pleasure he imagines it will give them both for many years to come.

"Do you like it?" he asks.

"Sure," Lisette says.

An hour later, though, after taking her first shower, Lisette doesn't look happy.

"The water pressure is weak," she grumbles.

"How can you focus on that?" Manuel asks. He can't believe Lisette is criticizing the new bathroom. The improvements are all there, undeniable.

"I'm just being honest," Lisette counters. "I care about functionality, not looks."

"Nothing I do is good enough for you!" Manuel yells and storms out of the room.

Manuel sits on their porch for a while, spinning a self-pity cycle. Then, he remembers the *yes, and* tool in her relationship first aid kit. *Yes,* he can love how things have turned out *and*...Lisette can focus on the water pressure. It's okay to be different. They *are* different. There is room for both of their priorities and perspectives.

"Sorry I got reactive," Manuel apologizes a few hours later. "I know you want the same water pressure as the old bathroom because you care about things working well."

With Manuel taking a *yes, and* approach, Lisette finds it easier to soften.

"Yes, and it makes sense that my complaining about the water pressure upsets you," she says, "especially after all the effort you put into making the bathroom look so good."

JOINT EXERCISE: Improvising with "Yes, And"

You and your partner sit or stand opposite each other. When you're both ready, the partner who will be the scene-starter speaks a single short sentence (no more than ten or fifteen words) out loud celebrating some aspect of their partner's character or personality.

For example, the scene-starter might say, "You're great with my friends." The other partner responds with "Yes, and," either following the theme introduced by the scene-starter or going off in a new direction while affirming the last statement—or, at the very least, not negating it. They might say, "Yes, and your friend Charlie asked us to meet him for dinner in a submarine." The scene-starter continues with a "yes, and" statement, drawing on what was said while introducing something new. It's fine if what you say doesn't make a whole lot of sense or sounds silly.

Here's a sample of how this might flow:

Partner A (scene-starter): *You're great with my friends.*

Partner B: *Yes, and your friend Charlie asked us to meet him for dinner in a submarine.*

Partner A: *Yes, and purple hats are a sign of intelligence.*

Partner B: *Yes, and I'm a genius.*

Partner A: *Yes, and maybe we should move to Canada.*

Partner B: *Yes, and winters are rough in Canada.*

JOINT EXERCISE: What We Learned Doing Improv

In a journal, write your answers to the questions listed below. When you're done, share your responses, referring to the Speaker and Listener responsibilities in the introduction for a refresher on creating safety and supporting connection.

* Was it easy or hard for you to affirm your partner's statements?

* Did you get caught up in the content of what your partner was saying?

* Did you have an impulse to contradict your partner, correct them, or start to worry about or overthink their statements?

Adaptability

Part of palliative care in a relationship is being adaptable. You recognize how you contribute to problems. You see how you hurt your partner through your stubbornness, impatience, poor self-care, self-centeredness, or other limitations, even when you have good intentions. When you disappoint or hurt your partner, you remain open to understanding them and their experience of what happened. After an argument or disagreement, if your partner looks sad or shut down, you ask, with genuine curiosity, "How have I hurt you?"

You can also listen and take in your partner's feedback, even if it's hard to hear. According to research done by couples therapist Dr. Gottman, only 31 percent of couples' problems are actually "solvable" (Gottman and Silver 2015). This means most couples live together without ever solving 69 percent of their problems. Couples who are happy have as many potentially conflict-generating differences as couples who are unhappy. What distinguishes these two types of couples is how they choose to think about and handle unsolvable problems.

If your conflicts revolve around having different likes or dislikes, approaches to timeliness or cleanliness, or comfort levels with freedom or structure, you learn more about your partner's preferences as a way of learning more about them. Although it's important to have your own opinions and remain true to yourself, welcoming your partner's perspective paves the way for new possibilities you may never have been open to before. When you welcome your partner's experience of something you experience totally differently, you're showing care, acceptance, and respect. You say things like, "Let me think about it," or "Give me some time to consider your point of view," rather than shooting down your partner's response, idea, dream, or desire. In the end, welcoming their perspective can expand your horizons on food, art, sports, hobbies, music, travel, people, culture, politics, and even your philosophy of life.

Balancing personal convictions with adaptability is a lifelong palliative-care practice. It won't be easy, smooth, or perfect. It's like juggling two different objects with different shapes and weights. In a relationship, the question becomes, "How can I be me and you be you without either of us winning or making the other person bad or wrong?"

If you can't or won't allow your partner to influence you, power struggles will interfere with your connection and closeness. On the other hand, if you're *too* flexible, you may end up stifling and neglecting yourself—and becoming passive-aggressive and resentful.

Although many of us may sometimes fantasize about a partner who shares our interests and preferences, not too many people would actually want to date or marry themselves. There's a reason the popular saying is "opposites attract" and not "clones attract." Adopting your partner's views, tastes, and preferences may reduce conflict, but it also reduces the dynamic energy in your relationship. Relationships challenge you to grow precisely *because* you and your partner are different.

Kindness

Like the other palliative relationship care skills, kindness tends to be needed most when it's hardest to give. When you're angry at one another or judging yourself harshly, be kind. Practice SLOW. See and label your ruminative thoughts and blame, worry, control, doubt, or self-pity cycles. Open to what's happening within you in the moment and welcome your vulnerabilities. Let your partner know you're going for a walk to clear your mind. Watch a candle flame, sing, dance, work out, look at the sky, listen to podcasts, read, write, paint, play frisbee, cook, snowboard, do sudoku puzzles, take a bath, and meditate or pray. Loving isn't easy, and you'll both make mistakes. It's okay to learn how to love gradually and imperfectly. Apply the balm of kindness to your experience of conflict, pain, or discomfort in your relationship.

Remember Eddie and Chandra from chapter 1? One Sunday afternoon, Eddie was putting on his running shoes while Chandra studied for an upcoming exam.

"Where are you going?" Chandra asked, her tone accusatory.

"For a run," Eddie said defensively.

"How come you never ask me to come with you?" Chandra asked.

When Eddie shared this incident in one of our therapy sessions, he sounded excited.

"I could see she was suffering," he admitted. "For the first time, instead of thinking about how our relationship was doomed, I took a breath and stayed open."

"Come on," Eddie remembers saying. "Get your shoes on. I'd love to run with you."

"No, go ahead by yourself," Chandra had responded darkly. "You'd rather go alone."

Chandra admitted it had been hard for her to accept Eddie's offer.

"I'd already slipped into a blame cycle," Chandra shrugged. "Blaming *myself*. I was already thinking, *God, I'm so needy. No wonder he doesn't like doing things with me. I give him a hard time about every little thing.*"

"I mean it. I'd love to go for a run with you," Eddie had insisted. "We'll have fun. Let's enjoy this beautiful day."

Eddie's kindness helped them both. Chandra resisted the undertow of her blame cycle pulling her away from Eddie. She put her shoes on, and they went for a run. Eddie's kindness helped Chandra be kinder to herself.

We all have good days and bad days. Even if you've practiced communication skills for years and you keep your relationship first aid kit handy at all times, bad moods, rumination cycles, and unpredictable events will blindside you. When they do, at any moment, you can always shift gears and make the choice to be kind to yourself and your partner.

Curative Care: Repair

Luckily, when your connection with your partner breaks, it will usually repair itself if you draw on relational tools that support healing. Over time and with practice, repair can happen quickly and completely, often resulting in an even stronger bond than you had before. The more you and your partner are able to successfully repair, the easier it is to trust one another, experience your resilience, and relax into the safety of your relationship field.

The curative care process of repairing after a break in connection draws on a combination of skills you've been learning about in this chapter such as conscious communication, emotional intelligence, problem solving, and adaptability.

Here are four additional principles and skills that can support your repair process with your partner:

1. Remember the good.

2. Take ownership.

3. Have empathy.

4. Make amends.

Remember the Good

I'm guessing it's easy for you to focus on what isn't working in your relationship. Most of us don't need help doing this. The reason we're so good at focusing on what's wrong is *not* because we're negative people who intentionally sabotage connection. It's because we're human beings with ancestors who survived by expecting the worst to happen when a twig snapped in the forest behind them. This "expecting the worst" tendency kept our ancestors alive longer than those well-meaning early humans who said, "Oh, don't worry. I'm sure it's nothing."

We all carry millennia of fear-based conditioning in our DNA.

We have a biological bias in favor of negative, bad, unsatisfying, or dangerous elements and aspects of reality. This bias has been called "the positive-negative asymmetry effect." Our brains are wired to focus on negative elements of our lives and relationships much more often than on positive ones (Baumeister et al. 2001). As a result, we're more easily convinced of negative possibilities. We're primed to pick up on things that go wrong.

Anxious overthinking in our relationships reinforces this asymmetry. Our default setting has been programmed to notice what's negative, or "bad," over what's positive, or "good," in ourselves and our partner.

Therapist and founder of the Relationship Institute Terry Real calls the skill of remembering the good "holding your relationship in high regard" (Real 1997). This skill requires you to remember what you love about your partnership even when you've been swept into the current of your biological conditioning.

If your partner is late to pick you up and you ruminate about all the other times they've been late, try counterbalancing the positive-negative asymmetry effect by appreciating their efforts and what they *are* doing for you. Recall when they *have* picked you up on time. Or else think about your partner's many positive characteristics. Reflect on recent times the two of you laughed, had fun, and comforted each other.

SOLO EXERCISE: My Good List

In a journal, write "My Good List" at the top of a page. Make a list of what you respect, love, and admire about your partner and value in your relationship (including good things you normally take for granted). List your partner's positive traits and loving actions and the quiet pleasures you share. You may recall William and Theo from chapter 1. Refer to William's list below for ideas.

Once you've created your Good List, keep it handy by your bed, in your wallet, or in a drawer where you can easily refer to it.

William's Good List

Theo sings in the shower.

He's cheerful and his presence comforts me.

I trust him.

He's loyal.

Our relationship is home.

He makes me coffee in the morning.

He accompanies me to medical appointments.

He encourages me when I'm feeling down.

He takes my hand on walks.

We are usually respectful toward each other.

He tries his best to listen.

His intentions are good.

He loves cooking for me.

He has a killer sense of humor.

Take Ownership

I have an old T-shirt my husband made for me over seventeen years ago, when we were dating. I keep it in the back of one of my dresser drawers. It's a memento from the earliest stages of our courtship, when we were both oblivious to the impact our rumination cycles had on our relationship field. We didn't even know a field existed or that we polluted it with our anxious overthinking and rumination cycles. We were deeply entrenched in our *Problem Partner Won't Change* dead-end script, thinking, *If only he/she would be more like me, this relationship might work.* We were trying to turn each other into our clone.

The T-shirt he made me reads: "Kiss me, I'm critical, demanding, irresponsible, and impatient."

I also made him a T-shirt.

It reads, "Kiss me, I'm rejecting, closed-minded, inflexible, and pessimistic."

You may be asking yourself, "Why in the world would you give a T-shirt like that to someone you love?"

Bear with me and read on. There's a method to this madness.

Whenever we had fights, I said things like, "Why are you so negative?" "Why can't you be more affectionate?" "You should trust life more." He said things like, "You're too demanding," "This is just the way I am," and "Stop controlling me."

Our relationship-improvement strategy of fighting, disconnecting, criticizing each other, and stonewalling wasn't working. It quickly became clear that we weren't going to make it unless we changed the plot of our love story ASAP.

After several months of weekly couples therapy and a lot of self-reflection, we recognized that we actually *did* have some of the negative qualities that had triggered so much defensiveness. We decided to "own" these qualities and take responsibility for them instead of getting offended each time our partner suggested we possessed them.

Hence, the his-and-her T-shirts from hell. Creating them together brought comic relief to our dead-end script. Receiving them from one another helped us take ourselves less seriously and practice humility. Sometimes, we put them on during a disagreement as a silent peace offering. They made us laugh.

Interestingly, the more we were able to own the negative traits on our shirts, the less we exhibited them. My husband became more optimistic, affectionate, and flexible. He also experienced me as being more understanding, responsible, and patient. We knew we had negative experiences of each other as well as positive ones—and this was okay. Each of us doing our own work to become a better partner ended up being easier than pressuring one another to change.

Taking ownership of all of who you are—including traits and characteristics you're not proud of—is serious business. Having fun with the process can help get you through tough times.

JOINT EXERCISE: Ownership T-Shirts

Get two broad-tipped Sharpie markers and two white T-shirts or undershirts. Alternatively, you can use pieces of paper and pin them to T-shirts you already have.

In a journal, each partner writes down two lists of ten adjectives. One is a list of adjectives describing some of your traits which are considered pleasant. The other is a list of adjectives describing your less-pleasant traits. If you find yourself stuck at any point as you think of pleasant or unpleasant adjectives, look at the other half of the list for inspiration. Come up with the opposite of either the pleasant or unpleasant adjective you've already written down.

Once you and your partner have two lists of your own pleasant and unpleasant adjectives, trade lists and place a star beside four of the pleasant traits on your partner's "pleasant adjectives" list. Place a star beside four traits on your partner's "unpleasant adjectives" list too. Then, give the lists back and write, "Kiss me, I'm…" followed by the four unpleasant traits your partner starred, either on the paper you'll be pinning or directly onto your T-shirt.

Put your T-shirts on and stand in front of each other or side by side in front of a mirror. If you like, you can also kiss each other (as per the instructions on the T-shirts).

For "Ownership T-Shirts" to be helpful and freeing, you'll need to see your own flaws without getting overwhelmed by shame or self-blame. You'll also need to connect with the higher purpose of this exercise and contain any impulse to criticize or shame each other.

If for whatever reason you're not comfortable making these T-shirts referencing unpleasant traits, you can still do the exercise with the four *pleasant* traits your partner starred on your list. Owning your pleasant traits can support the self-esteem and confidence you'll need to own your unpleasant traits at some point in the future.

Your lists might look something like this:

Pleasant	Unpleasant
Kind	Grouchy
Thoughtful	Thoughtless
Optimistic	Pessimistic
Hardworking	Irresponsible
Forgiving	Perfectionistic
Understanding	Punishing
Trusting	Controlling
Caring	Self-Absorbed
Loving	Cynical
Hopeful	Hostile

Have Empathy

Empathy is one of the most powerful curative care tools you can have in your relationship first aid kit. Although it's an essential ingredient in the curative care of any relationship, it can't be faked or forced. You can't administer it like a Band-Aid, tearing it from its antiseptic sleeve and slapping it onto an emotional scrape or cut. Empathy is a movement of the heart. It happens when you open yourself to what another person is experiencing and wholeheartedly keep them company where they are. When rumination cycles no longer block your vulnerabilities, this heart-movement can arise naturally.

We've already talked about different conditions and skills that promote empathy: healthy thinking, emotional intelligence, conscious communication, remembering the good, and taking ownership, to name a few. The more you engage in relationship-care skills, like *being with* what's happening rather than overthinking it, the more naturally occurring empathy can arise.

Make Amends

When you're sorry for something hurtful you've said or done, making amends with your partner "puts your money where your mouth is." It's how you translate conscious communication, ownership, and empathy into an action.

If you arrive late to a special dinner your partner planned and made, you can make amends by inviting your partner out for another special dinner soon afterward. If you took the wind out of your partner's sails with a pessimistic comment about one of their accomplishments, you can make amends with a small but thoughtful gift. If you were anxious at a time when your partner needed support, you can apologize and tell them how important they are to you.

How do you know what would constitute making amends after a conflict or period of disconnection? Many people make this step harder than it has to be by trying to guess, assume, or read their partner's mind—or by expecting their partner to be a mind-reader. Once you've listened to your partner, understood their perspective, and expressed remorse for your part in a disconnection, ask them: "How can I make it up to you?" Then, wait for their response. If you're on the other side of this dynamic, and your partner doesn't know how to make amends, tell them.

They may want a hug. They may want verbal reassurance, such as "I'm lucky I'm with you" or "What you think matters a lot." They may ask you to do something related to what triggered the conflict. If possible, do what they ask promptly, generously, and sincerely.

If your partner asks you, "How can I make it up to you?" identify something your partner could do that would help *you* move on. When they do it, take it in. Receive it. Don't sabotage their gift by disapproving of it. Allow it to soften your heart. Resentment isn't good for either of you. If you have trouble taking in your partner's attempts at making amends, notice your thinking. Are you in a rumination cycle? Practice SLOW to understand your resistance better.

You have a right to ask for what you want. Don't minimize your wants or second-guess them. Make a clear request of your partner. "I'd like a tight, ten-second hug." "Block that guy on social media." "Write me a haiku about when we first met." "Paint my toenails." "Include me in your parenting decisions with our kids." Ask for what you want with gusto. Ask without caretaking your partner. Then let go of whatever happens next. Give your partner the space to figure out whether, how, and when to give you what you asked for.

Your partner can say no if they're not ready, able, or willing to fulfill your request. They can also say maybe. Don't let your fear of a negative response prevent you from honoring what you want and asking for it. Every time you connect with yourself enough to recognize and express a true need, it's a small win, regardless of whether your need gets met. When your partner lets you know something you can do to make amends and reconnect, it's a gift.

JOINT EXERCISE: Our Relationship First Aid Kit

In a journal, you and your partner will each write down five or six "items" from the list below that you would like to use when you're ruminating, disconnected from one another, misunderstanding each other, or working through a conflict. Once you've written out your lists, notice which items you've both selected. Copy these items onto a separate sheet of paper under the heading: "Our Relationship First Aid Kit." Make copies of this list, one for each of you.

Keep this list of preventive, palliative, and curative care strategies handy. Add additional items to your list as you recognize which ones might help in new situations. Review the items regularly. When you're struggling, upset, or disconnected—or when something seems off balance between you—use one or more of the items from your first aid kit.

Relationship First Aid Kit Items

Practice conscious communication.

Review Speaker and Listener responsibilities.

See and label rumination cycles.

Open to the vulnerability trio: sensations, emotions, and impulses.

Welcome whatever arises without judgment.

Practice acceptance in blame cycles.

Release perfectionism and what I can't control in control cycles.

Connect with my body in the here and now in worry cycles.

Work on my capacity to wisely trust in doubt cycles.

Take responsibility for my contribution to problems and challenges in self-pity cycles.

Remind myself: "If this thing I fear transpires the way I would like it to, that would be great. If it doesn't, that will be okay too, because either way, I am and will be okay."

Cultivate a growth mindset.

Remember: "I can trust life to unfold in my own best interest in its own timing."

Remember: "I can learn, have, and enjoy more by relaxing my grip on the outcome I had in mind and receiving the positive in what's arriving now."

Remember: "Things can be interesting and valuable even if they're not what I expect."

Plug up the leaks—energetic, toxic omissions, and expressive.

Review our ASP and get clear on small things we can do to practice secure attachment.

Practice SLOW on the spot.

Practice SLOW after the fact.

Practice SLOW alone.

Go through a SLOW joint process together.

Review my Warning Lights List.

Review and add to My Small Wins List.

Get grounded in one breath.

Reframe my partner's "critical" feedback as a cue for overthinking.

See dead-end scripts.

Rewrite the plot of our script.

Review our triggers.

Label thoughts using vulnerable language.

Review attachment fears to cultivate self-compassion.

Use awareness anchors.

Use an adult time-out.

Welcome what's happening in the here and now.

Choose a healthy thinking alternative to overthinking.

After an argument or disagreement, ask "How have I hurt you?"

Say, "Let me think about it" or "Give me some time to consider your
   point of view."

Be kinder to myself and to my partner.

Read through my Good List.

Add new items to my Good List.

Make, remake, or wear my ownership T-shirt.

Adopt a *yes, and* approach.

Practice taking ownership.

Practice repairing after conflicts and misunderstandings.

Have empathy.

Make amends.

Preventive, palliative, and curative care strategies can help you avoid problems, relieve suffering, and heal in your relationship. In contrast to rumination, healthy thinking offers a form of preventive care that brings couples' perceptions into alignment with their inner experiences and the world around them. Adaptive self-reflection, metacognition, emotional intelligence, problem solving, and positive reappraisal are examples of healthy thinking. Some basic but important palliative care tools you can use in your relationship are conscious communication, adult time-outs, the "yes, and" approach, adaptability, and kindness. Repair is one of the most powerful curative care tools in relationships. It involves remembering the good, taking ownership, having empathy, and making amends.

Conclusion

One of the most basic human rights we have is our right to be ourselves. Everyone deserves to be themselves deeply and truly. Even when you've been raised in a culture that prioritizes thinking over your many other amazing human skills and capacities, you still deserve an opportunity to learn how to be you—and how to *be with* what's happening within you in the here and now. You have a right to explore what's hidden under the buffer of your relationship rumination and anxious overthinking so you can embody your own robust aliveness. This is where happier love stories begin: with the choice to be with yourself as you are and experience yourself fully.

Our love stories are like choose-your-own-adventure novels. In love, you make important choices every day that will either take the plot of your story in the direction you want or off course, in a direction you don't want. One choice will carry you to a page where your adventure builds and deepens. Another choice, sometimes on the same day—or even a few moments later—takes you to a page where your passionate, exciting adventure ends prematurely. Your choices influence the choices that follow, and your new choices influence the ones that follow that. This choose-your-own-adventure principle underlies all our love stories.

So what will *you* choose? Which page will you turn to?

In this book, you've gotten to know love's quiet enemy: relationship rumination. Engaged in by one or both partners within a committed, romantic bond, chronic, repetitive, negative thinking is especially damaging when it's hidden and unacknowledged. You've explored how it interferes with your satisfaction with your partner and your relationship. You and your partner have been looking at rumination through a different lens, directing your attention inward when you experience a trigger rather than outward onto what triggered you. You've been seeing your thoughts and rumination cycles. You've been labeling your mental patterns and opening to what's underneath. You've been welcoming more of who you are, even when it's been uncomfortable. By recognizing what makes overthinking hard to spot and how rumination cycles get activated, you've been shining a light onto blame, control, doubt, worry, and self-pity cycles.

What makes a love story an adventure? A lot of things, but most of all, the exhilaration of any adventure comes from the fact that no true, wild, tender, vibrant experience can be known and predicted. Every single love story unfolds in its own unforeseeable, unique way. It evolves and develops, surprising even the people in it. The people in love stories are undeniably who they are—one-of-a-kind, wonderful, complicated, evolving, imperfect, and maddening too at times. They combine physical, spiritual, genetic, emotional, ancestral, and cognitive gifts and vulnerabilities. People in love stories aren't automatons bounced around by thoughts like pinballs in a pinball machine. They write their love stories together with each choice they make. Each choice turns the page. The small, consistent choices shape love—sometimes more than the big ones.

Whatever choices you make in *your* choose-your-own-adventure love story, you are better poised to embrace life around you and within you when you see yourselves as participants in a vibrant, responsive relationship field—a shifting, energetic ebb and flow of connectivity. Working toward interdependence, healthy boundaries, and safety in your field is a collaboration. Every great collaboration starts with doing your part while keeping the overarching goal in mind.

How will *you* do your part to shape your love story? Will you strengthen your *being with* muscles, pausing to experience what lies beyond your rumination? Will you look at the ways early attachment experiences with primary caregivers have influenced your needs and fears related to closeness and distance? Will you consider your ASP in moments when you and your partner are struggling—and then do one small thing that stretches you into greater security and trust? Will you recognize when you're reciting the same old lines of a familiar dead-end script? Will you use SLOW regularly—alone or with your partner, on the spot or after the fact—fostering a growth mindset long after you've returned this book to a bookshelf or moved on to a new book on your digital device? When you can shift your mindset from fixed to growth, seeing your relationship as a cocreated field, being with and welcoming yourself and your partner as you truly are in the here and now, rumination weakens. That's a win. Love can flourish.

Breaking the cycle of anxious rumination doesn't happen by accident. It's not magic. It happens one thought, trigger, and day at a time, one choice at a time, through seeing, labeling, opening, and welcoming. It happens when you keep your relationship first aid kit handy and well-stocked with preventive, palliative, and curative relationship-care tools and skills. Pull out and use the items in your kit regularly. Don't let them gather dust. Use them to nurture love. You and your partner are built to grow together, welcoming yourselves and each other more fully as you are right now in your relationship field. You don't have to overthink it.

Acknowledgments

Livia Kent, you planted the seed for this book when you invited me to write for the *Psychotherapy Networker*. I'm grateful to Wendy Millstine, acquisitions editor at New Harbinger, for reaching out to me after reading one of my articles. Elizabeth Hollis Hansen and Jennifer Holder provided the right balance of freedom and guidance as I developed the manuscript. Gretel Hakanson, your generosity and attention to detail made the final phases of this book's creation a pleasure. Rita Rosenkranz, my agent, guided me with practical advice at key moments, reducing my own anxious overthinking.

I'm indebted to Steve Shapiro as a clinician, teacher, and supervisor for transforming how I think about anxiety and defenses—and how I work with clients. To the members of the 2019–2022 Malvern Core Training group—thank you for being on the ride with me.

I'm grateful to all my clients, therapists, coaches, supervisors, teachers, and colleagues—including Carol Kramer, Dianne Modell, Linda Carroll, and Jeffrey Frank—for challenging and inspiring me, sharing yourselves, and shaping my thinking about thinking and being.

To the people who read my books, articles, newsletters, Instagram posts, and blogs—thank you for your resonance. I'm grateful to have you on the receiving end of the words I put on the page and screen. It's how these words land and gestate within you that gives them their true value.

Paula Salguero, our conversations about love, vulnerability, and motherhood at ten o'clock at night watching our sons do inverts and layback airs got me through the many long months of a global pandemic. Our friendship enriches me more than I can express. Po Hong-Yu, your steady encouragement over the course of this project helped me do it my way. Dyan Machan, eternal adventuress, thank you for the magic you continue bringing to my life. Pat Muñoz, aka Mom, all those fresh garden vegetables you delivered while I wrote and revised these pages meant the world to me. John Muñoz, you're the best brother a sister could wish for. Thank you for being with me from the beginning.

References

Bartholomew, K., and L. M. Horowitz. 1991. "Attachment Styles Among Young Adults: A Test of a Four-Category Model." *Journal of Personality and Social Psychology* 61, no. 2: 226–244.

Baucom, D. H., N. B. Epstein, J. S. Kirby, and J. J. LaTaillade. 2015. "Cognitive-Behavioral Couple Therapy." In *Clinical Handbook of Couple Therapy*, 5th ed., edited by A. S. Gurman, J. L. Lebow, and D. K. Snyder, 23–60. New York: Guilford Press.

Baumeister, R. F., E. Bratslavsky, C. Finkenauer, and K. D. Vohs. 2001. "Bad Is Stronger than Good." *Review of General Psychology* 5, no. 4: 323–370. https://doi.org/10.1037/1089-2680.5.4.323.

Berns, G. S., J. Chappelow, M. Cekic, C. F. Zink, G. Pagnoni, and M. E. Martin-Skurski. 2006. "Neurobiological Substrates of Dread." *Science* 312, no. 5774 (May 5): 754–758.

Bowlby, J. 1969. *Attachment and Loss*. New York: Basic Books.

Buber, M. 2010. *I and Thou*. CT: Martino Publishing.

Brown, B. 2012. *Daring Greatly: How the Courage to Be Vulnerable Transforms the Way We Live, Love, Parent, and Lead*. New York: Avery.

Caron, A., M.-F. Lafontaine, J.-F. Bureau, C. Levesque, and S. M. Johnson. 2012. "Comparisons of Close Relationships: An Evaluation of Relationship Quality and Patterns of Attachment to Parents, Friends, and Romantic Partners in Young Adults." *Canadian Journal of Behavioral Science/Revue Canadienne des Sciences du Comportement*. 44, no. 4: 245–256.

Carver, C. S., and M. F. Scheier. 2012. "Cybernetic Control Processes and the Self-Regulation of Behavior." In *The Oxford Handbook of Human Motivation*, edited by R. M. Ryan, 28–42. New York: Oxford University Press.

Carver, C. S., and M. F. Scheier. 2013. "Self-Regulation of Action and Affect." In *Handbook of Self-Regulation: Research, Theory, and Applications*, 2nd ed., edited by K. D. Vohs and R. F. Baumeister, 3–21. New York: Guilford Press.

Christensen, A., S. Dimidjian, and C. R. Martell. 2015. "Integrative Behavioral Couple Therapy." In *Clinical Handbook of Couple Therapy*, 5th ed., edited by A. S. Gurman, J. L. Lebow, and D. K. Snyder, 61–94. New York: Guilford Press.

Cowen, A., and D. Keltner. 2017. "Varieties of Reported Emotional Experience," *Proceedings of the National Academy of Sciences* 114, no. 38.

Dana, D. 2018. *The Polyvagal Theory in Therapy: Engaging the Rhythm of Regulation.* New York: W. W. Norton & Company.

Das, K. 2020. "Scientific Study on the Particle Nature of Thoughts—Do Thoughts Matter and Mass!!!" In *Current Topics in Medicine and Medical Research* vol. 2, edited by S. K. Jain. West Bengal, India: PB International.

Du Maurier, D. 1800. *Rebecca.* William Morrow Paperbacks.

Dweck, C. S. 2007. *Mindset: The New Psychology of Success: How We Can Learn to Fulfill Our Potential.* New York: Ballantine Books.

Eckman, P. 2007. *Emotions Revealed: Recognizing Face and Feelings to Improve Communication and Emotional Life.* New York: Owl Books.

Epstein, M. 2013. *Thoughts Without a Thinker: Psychotherapy from a Buddhist Perspective.* New York: Basic Books.

Fraenkel, P. 2009. "The Therapeutic Palette: A Guide to Choice Points in Integrative Couple Therapy." *Clinical Social Work Journal* 37: 234–247.

Frederickson, J. 2017. *The Lies We Tell Ourselves: How to Face the Truth, Accept Yourself, and Create a Better Life.* Kansas City, MO: Seven Leaves Press.

Gottman, J., and N. Silver. 2015. *The Seven Principles for Making Marriage Work.* New York: Harmony Books.

Grof, S., and C. Grof. 2010. *Holotropic Breathwork: A New Approach to Self-Exploration and Therapy.* Albany: State University of New York Press.

Hanson, R., and F. Hanson. 2018. *Resilient: How to Grow an Unshakable Core of Calm, Strength, and Happiness.* New York: Harmony.

Hendrix, H., and H. L. Hunt. 1992. *Keeping the Love You Find: A Guide for Singles.* New York: Atria.

Hicks, T. 2018. *Embodied Conflict: The Neural Basis of Conflict and Communication.* New York: Routledge.

Howes, R. 2021. "Total Liberation: A Buddhist Approach to Healing." *Psychotherapy Networker* (November–December): 75–76.

Jenkins, A. 2017. "Which Is Safer: Airplanes or Cars?" *Fortune* Magazine, July.

Johnson, S. 2008. *Hold Me Tight: Seven Conversations for a Lifetime of Love*. New York: Little Brown.

Katie, B. 2002. *Loving What Is: Four Questions That Can Change Your Life*. New York: Harmony Books.

Keller, H. 1940. *Let Us Have Faith*. New York: Doubleday, Doran, and Co.

Kinderman, P., M. Schwannauer, E. Pontin, and S. Tai. 2013. "Psychological Processes Mediate the Impact of Familial Risk, Social Circumstances and Life Events on Mental Health." *PLOS ONE* 8, no. 10.

Levine, P. 1997. *Waking the Tiger: Healing Trauma: The Innate Capacity to Transform Overwhelming Experiences*. Berkeley, CA: North Atlantic Books.

Levine, A., and R. Heller. 2010. *Attached: The New Science of Adult Attachment and How It Can Help You Find—and Keep—Love*. New York: Random House.

Li, J., D. E. Osher, H. A. Hansen, and Z. M. Saygin. 2020. "Innate Connectivity Patterns Drive the Development of the Visual Word Form Area." *Scientific Reports* 10: 18039.

Lipton, B. 2015. *The Biology of Belief: Unleashing the Power of Consciousness, Matter, and Miracles*, 10th ed. New York: Hay House.

Markman, H., S. Stanley, and S. Blumberg. 2010. *Fighting for Your Marriage, A Deluxe Revised Edition of the Classic Bestseller for Enhancing Marriage and Preventing Divorce*, 3rd ed. San Francisco: Jossey-Bass.

Mennin, D. S., and D. M. Fresco. 2013. "What, Me Worry and Ruminate About *DSM-5* and RDoC? The Importance of Targeting Negative Self-Referential Processing." *Clinical Psychology: Science and Practice* 20, no. 3: 258–267. https://doi.org/10.1111/cpsp.12038.

Nagoski, E. 2015. *Come as You Are: The Surprising New Science That Will Transform Your Sex Life*. New York: Simon & Schuster.

Nagoski, E., and A. Nagoski. 2019. *Burnout: The Secret to Unlocking the Stress Cycle*. New York: Ballantine Books.

Nestor, J. 2020. *Breath: The New Science of a Lost Art*. New York: Penguin.

Neubauer, S., J. Hublin, and P. Gunz. 2018. "The Evolution of Modern Human Brain Shape." *Science Advances* 4, no. 1 (January 24).

Nhat Hanh, T. 2002. *No Death, No Fear: Comforting Wisdom for Life*. New York: Penguin Books.

Nolen-Hoeksema, S. 2003. *Women Who Think Too Much: How to Break Free of Overthinking and Reclaim Your Life.* New York: St. Martin's Griffin.

Nuru, I. 2020. *You're So Patient with Me.* Middletown, DE: Independently published.

Pittman, C. M., and E. M. Karle. 2015. *Rewire Your Anxious Brain: How to Use the Neuroscience of Fear to End Anxiety, Panic, and Worry.* Oakland, CA: New Harbinger Publications.

Querstret, D., and M. Cropley. 2013. "Assessing Treatments Used to Reduce Rumination and/or Worry: A Systematic Review." *Clinical Psychology Review* 33, no 8: 996–1009.

Real, T. 1997. *I Don't Want to Talk About It.* New York: Scribner.

Real, T. 2007. *The New Rules of Marriage: What You Need to Know to Make Love Work.* New York: Ballantine Books.

Sapolsky, R. 2017. *Behave: The Biology of Humans at Our Best and Worst.* New York, Penguin Books.

Shapiro, F. 2014. "I Was Wrong About the Origin of the Serenity Prayer." *Huffington Post.* https://huffpost.com/entry/serenity-prayer-origin_n_5331924.

Shapiro, S. 2019. "Transforming Resistance Fall Retreat: Working with the Challenges of Defense and Anxiety to Promote Rapid Therapeutic Change." (Workshop, November 4–7. Malvern, PA.)

Shapiro, S. 2021. Core Training lecture, "Understanding components of affect and affect facilitation." (Webinar.)

Smith, D. 2001. "Multitasking Undermines Our Efficiency, Study Suggests." *Monitor on Psychology* 32, no. 9 (October). http://www.apa.org/monitor/oct01/multitask.

Tawwab, N. G. 2021. *Set Boundaries, Find Peace: A Guide to Reclaiming Yourself.* London, England: Piatkus.

Tolle, E. 2008. *A New Earth: Awakening to Your Life's Purpose.* New York: Penguin Books.

Tseng, J., and J. Poppenk. 2020. "Brain Meta-State Transitions Demarcate Thoughts Across Task Contexts Exposing the Mental Noise of Trait Neuroticism." *Nature Communications* 11: 3480.

Young, J. E., J. S. Klosko, and M. E. Weishaar. 2003. *Schema Therapy: A Practitioner's Guide.* New York: Guilford Press.

Alicia Muñoz, LPC, is a certified couples therapist, and author of three relationship books. Over the past fifteen years, she has provided individual, group, and couples therapy in clinical settings, including Bellevue Hospital in New York, NY. Muñoz currently works as a couples counselor in private practice. She connects with her readers and followers through monthly blogs, newsletters, podcasts, and radio shows, as well as through Instagram at @aliciamunozcouples, and Facebook and Twitter at @aliciamunozlpc. Muñoz is a member of the Washington School of Psychiatry, the American Psychological Association, and the Mid-Atlantic Association of Imago and Relationship Therapists. She is also an expert contributor to *Psychotherapy Networker*, www.mind bodygreen.com, and other print and online magazines. You can learn more about her at www.aliciamunoz.com.

Foreword writer **Linda Carroll, LMFT**, is a psychotherapist, workshop presenter, and author of numerous books, including *Love Cycles* and *Love Skills*. She speaks frequently on the subject of relationship communication throughout the US and Mexico.

Real change *is* possible

For more than forty-five years, New Harbinger has published proven-effective self-help books and pioneering workbooks to help readers of all ages and backgrounds improve mental health and well-being, and achieve lasting personal growth. In addition, our spirituality books offer profound guidance for deepening awareness and cultivating healing, self-discovery, and fulfillment.

Founded by psychologist Matthew McKay and Patrick Fanning, New Harbinger is proud to be an independent, employee-owned company. Our books reflect our core values of integrity, innovation, commitment, sustainability, compassion, and trust. Written by leaders in the field and recommended by therapists worldwide, New Harbinger books are practical, accessible, and provide real tools for real change.

 **newharbinger**publications

MORE BOOKS from
NEW HARBINGER PUBLICATIONS

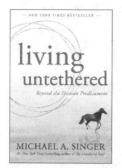

Did you know there are **free tools** you can download for this book?

Free tools are things like **worksheets**, **guided meditation exercises**, and **more** that will help you get the most out of your book.

You can download free tools for this book— whether you bought or borrowed it, in any format, from any source—from the New Harbinger website. All you need is a NewHarbinger.com account. Just use the URL provided in this book to view the free tools that are available for it. Then, click on the "download" button for the free tool you want, and follow the prompts that appear to log in to your NewHarbinger.com account and download the material.

You can also save the free tools for this book to your **Free Tools Library** so you can access them again anytime, just by logging in to your account! Just look for this button on the book's free tools page.

+ Save this to my free tools library